# COMPUTER
# MUSIC
# PROJECTS

## OTHER BOOKS OF INTEREST

# COMPUTER MUSIC PROJECTS

by

## R.A. PENFOLD

**BERNARD BABANI (publishing) LTD**
**THE GRAMPIANS**
**SHEPHERDS BUSH ROAD**
**LONDON W6 7NF**
**ENGLAND**

# PLEASE NOTE

Although every care has been taken with the production of this book to ensure that any projects, designs, modifications and/or programs etc. contained herewith, operate in a correct and safe manner and also that any components specified are normally available in Great Britain, the Publishers do not accept responsibility in any way for the failure, including fault in design, of any project, design, modification or program to work correctly or to cause damage to any other equipment that it may be connected to or used in conjunction with, or in respect of any other damage or injury that may be so caused, nor do the Publishers accept responsibility in any way for the failure to obtain specified components.

Notice is also given that if equipment that is still under warranty is modified in any way or used or connected with home-built equipment then that warranty may be void.

© 1985 BERNARD BABANI (publishing) LTD

First Published – November 1885

British Library Cataloguing in Publication Data
Penfold, R.A.
    Computer music projects.——(BP; 173)
    1. Computer composition
    I. Title
    781.6′1′02854044    MT56

ISBN 0 85934 147 X

Printed and Bound in Great Britain by Cox & Wyman Ltd, Reading

# Preface

Computers have great potential for revolutionising many aspects of our lives, but outside the realms of business and games their impact, as yet, has been rather limited in most fields. One definite exception is in the area of electronic music, and over the recent years many types of electronic instrument and effects unit have changed almost beyond recognition with the introduction of ever more complex digital circuitry. This gives the user more and more features, but fortunately not at ever increasing cost, and today's instruments represent outstanding value for money. Of course, it is not essential to stay within the confines of the commercial "black boxes", and modern electronic instruments leave great scope for the experimenter. A suitable home computer plus some home constructed hardware and a ready made electronic instrument of some kind can provide an immensely versatile system, effectively making the instrument at the centre of the system even more outstanding value for money.

The purpose of this book is to show some of the ways in which a home computer can be used to good effect in the production of electronic music. Topics covered include sequencing and control via analogue and MIDI interfaces, computers as digital delay lines, and sound generators for computer control. Everything has been kept as simple and jargon-free as possible, but it has necessarily been assumed that the reader has at least a small amount of experience with computer software and techniques, and at constructing simple electronic projects. This book is not aimed at complete beginners, but on the other hand it should not be necessary to have an advanced understanding of computer programming and hardware in order to build and use the circuits described here.

*R. A. Penfold*

# CONTENTS

# Chapter 1

## ANALOGUE INTERFACING

Even in the pre-digital days sythesisers could still be connected
together so that one instrument could be used to control another.
This was achieved using the gate in/out and CV in/out sockets.
Although not intended to give a means of computer control, these
sockets do in fact permit this. There are now very few new
instruments which have conventional gate and CV (control
voltage) inputs, but there are plenty of these instruments around
(and available quite cheaply second hand if you do not already
have access to one). Either a polyphonic or a monophonic
synthesiser in conjunction with a home computer and a suitable
interface can produce excellent results. Long sequences of notes
can easily be accommodated by the memories of most home
computers. Alternatively, bearing in mind that most synthesisers
can generate quite good percussive sounds, using a short loop
program the system can act as a rhythm generator.

### Control Signals

The gate output signal is usually in the form of a standard logic
signal which is at a very low voltage (typically 0.8 volts or less)
under stand-by conditions, but which goes to around +4 to +5
volts when a key is operated. Some synthesisers have a simple
envelope generator of the attack/decay type rather than of the full
ADSR variety, and with these the gate in/out sockets are normally
replaced with trigger in/out sockets. The difference between the
two types of signal is that the gate signal goes positive for as long as
a key is depressed, whereas the trigger signal only goes positive
for a few milliseconds each time a key is depressed, with the length
of key depression having no effect whatever on the trigger pulse
duration. Trigger outputs can often operate reasonably well
connected to gate inputs, and vice versa, although usable results
will not necessarily be obtained in every case. However, as far as
computer control is concerned there is no difficulty and a
computer can generate a suitable control pulse for use with either
type of input.

   Not all synthesisers use standard 5 volt logic levels, although in
some cases they will respond properly to 5 volt logic signals
anyway. In some cases though, the 5 volt control signals from the
computer must be converted to 0 and +15 volt logic levels (or

whatever) in order to give reliable triggering. We will return to this topic later.

The control voltage takes two standard forms. In some synthesisers (mainly the older types) the VCOs are linear types. In other words there is a linear relationship between control-voltage and output frequency, and if 1 volt gave (say) a 100Hz output, 2 volts would give 200Hz, 3 volts would give 300Hz, and so on. Most (probably all) synthesisers of current or recent manufacture use logarithmic VCOs, and the standard system has a 1 volt per octave law. For example, if 1 volt gave a 100Hz output frequency, 2 volts would produce 200Hz, 3 volts would produce 400Hz, 4 volts would give an 800Hz output, and so on.

This second method is very convenient from the computer control point of view. The keyboard generates a series of control voltages using a series of resistors in an attenuator circuit, and all the resistors have the same value. The basic arrangement used is shown in Figure 1, although only a few switches and resistors are used here, whereas in practice there would normally be a minimum of around thirty of each. The variable voltage source is adjusted so that the keyboard gives the correct voltage for each note, or 1 volt per twelve notes. This works out at 83.33 millivolts per note.

A digital to analogue converter gives an output voltage that increments in a linear fashion, and it therefore gives a series of output voltages that are essentially the same as those provided by the keyboard. In fact a typical digital to analogue converter provides an output which increments in quite small steps, and resolutions of around 10 millivolts are common. However, a variable gain DC amplifier can be used to step up the output voltages to match those provided by the keyboard. As a matter of interest, some analogue synthesisers use a "digitally scanned" keyboard. With this type of instrument the keyboard circuit does not have the standard potential divider circuit, but instead it is scanned by a digital circuit that detects which key (if any) has been pressed, and then feeds the appropriate number to a digital to analogue converter. The converter then generates the appropriate voltage and feeds it to the VCOs. This may seem to be an unnecessarily complex way of doing things, but synthesisers of this type often have some form of built-in digital controller, even if it is only a fairly basic type, and do not use this system just for the sake of it. It is sometimes possible to control a synthesiser of this type direct from a suitable computer port without the need for any

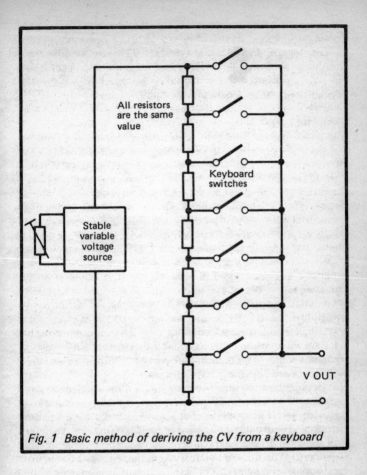

All resistors are the same value

Keyboard switches

Stable variable voltage source

V OUT

*Fig. 1 Basic method of deriving the CV from a keyboard*

form of interface, but this is likely to involve delving into the computer's interior, and unless you are sure you know what you are doing it might be better to control the unit via the CV input and a suitable interface.

Synthesisers which have a linear CV characteristic can not be easily controlled from a computer using the types of digital to analogue converter that are available to amateur users. These instruments do not have equal voltage increments from one note to the next, but instead have an increment size that increases as the output frequency increases. In theory it should be possible to obtain satisfactory results using an ordinary converter plus a linear to logarithmic voltage converter, but I have never managed to obtain good results using this method and a couple of colleagues who tried this sytem faired no better. It is a subject which will not be considered further here.

**Computer Ports**

The exact type of interface required depends on the type of computer port to which the interface must connect. Things are very much easier with computers such as the VIC-20 and BBC model B, which have a proper user port with input/output lines, than they are with a machine that has an expansion port where devices must be interfaced direct onto the computer's buses. For some computers (the Sinclair ZX81 and ZX Spectrum for instance), add-on parallel ports which provide a number of digital inputs and outputs are available (at the time this was written anyway). If you have a computer with only an expansion port, but a parallel interface board is available for it, I would strongly recommend the use of the interface as it will almost certainly make interfacing the unit to music circuits very much more straightforward. If you have only limited experience of electronics and computer interfacing I would **strongly advise against** trying to interface circuits direct to the computer's buses. Either use a computer which has a built-in user port or a ready made parallel interface board with one which does not.

It is not possible here to give an in-depth discussion of interfacing to all the home computers ever produced, but a few basics on interfacing some of the more popular (and for our purposes, more suitable) computers will be provided. Starting with the VIC-20 computer, this has the user port connections of Figure 2(a). The +5 volt line is an important one, and one which most computers can provide. It is important as it enables many types of interface and add-on to be powered from the computer without the need for any other power source. The other lines of principal intereset are PB0 to PB7. These are general purpose input/output lines, and they latch when used as outputs.

When using these lines the first task is to set them as inputs or outputs, as required. They do not all have to be set to the same mode, and each line is individually programmable as an input or an output. The data direction register is used to set each line to the desired operating mode, and in the VIC-20 this is at address

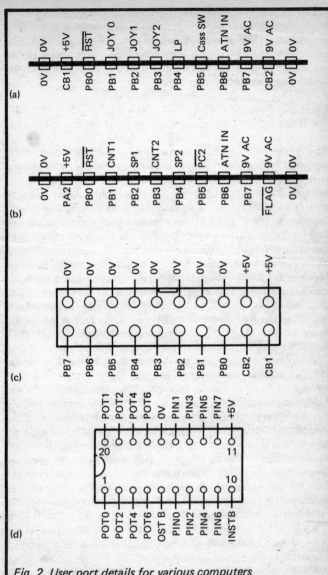

Fig. 2 User port details for various computers

36138. Each bit of the data direction register controls the corresponding line of the user port, and setting a bit to 1 designates its line as an output, setting it to 0 designates it as an input. If you are not familiar with the binary numbering system this can be a little confusing, but the table provided here should help to simplify matters.

| Line | PB0 | PB1 | PB2 | PB3 | PB4 | PB5 | PB6 | PB7 |
|------|-----|-----|-----|-----|-----|-----|-----|-----|
| Number | 1 | 2 | 4 | 8 | 16 | 32 | 64 | 128 |

This shows the number (in the ordinary decimal numbering system) that must be written to the data direction register in order to set each line as an output. The number required to set a line as an input is always zero. The lines are controlled simultaneously by writing a single value to the data direction register. This number is easy to calculate, and it is just a matter of first working out the eight numbers needed to set each line to the desired state, and then calculating the sum of these numbers. Rationalising things a little, decide which lines are to be outputs, look up the numbers for these lines in the above table, and add them together. In many cases either all the lines will be set as inputs (a DDR value of 0) or they will all be set as outputs (a DDR value of 255). The value is written to the data direction register using the POKE instruction (e.g. POKE 37138,255 would set all the lines as outputs). Incidentally, initially the lines are all in the input mode.

An important point to realise is that the data direction register is only used to set lines as inputs or outputs, and it is not used when writing data to or reading data from the lines. This is achieved using the peripheral register, and in the VIC-20 this is at address 37136. Writing 1 to a bit of the peripheral register sets the corresponding user port line high (about +5 volts), and writing 0 to a bit sets the corresponding line low (about 0 volts). If you are not familiar with the binary numbering system you can again use the table given earlier to work out the value required to set the lines to the desired states when they are used as outputs. For example, to set PB0 to PB3 high and the other four lines low would require a value of 15 (1+2+4+8=15). From BASIC "POKE 37136,15" would set the required output states. When reading input lines the PEEK function is used (e.g. PRINT PEEK(37136)).

Figure 2(b) shows connection details for the user port of the Commodore 64 computer. This is very similar to the VIC-20's user port, and if only the 5 volt supply and eight bit input/output are required it is in fact identical. Incidentally, connections to both computers are made via 2 by 12 way 0.156 inch female edge connectors. It is unlikely that you will be able to obtain a suitably polarised connector, and care must therefore be taken to always fit the connector the right way round. Note that although the VIC-20 and Commodore 64 computers have what are for most purposes hardware compatible user ports, they are slightly different from the software point of view. The only differences that are of significance for our present purposes are the data direction register and peripheral register addresses. These are 56579 and 56577 respectively.

The BBC model B computer has a user port which is very similar to those of the two Commodore machines, and connection details are given in Figure 2(c). The data direction register is at address &FE62 while the port itself is at address &FE60. BBC BASIC does not include PEEK and POKE as such, but a "?" is used to denote that a number is an address. Thus "?&FE62= 255" would set the data direction register to a value of 255 and would set all eight lines as outputs. To read the user port lines "PRINT ?&FE60" would be used. A 20 way IDC header socket is used to make the connection to the user port of the BBC machine.

Not all computers have a user port that is a direct equivalent to those on the Commodore and BBC machines. The MTX500 and MTX512 computers have a user port in the form of a 20 pin DIL integrated circuit holder on the printed circuit board. A slit at the rear of the case enables a ribbon cable to pass through the case to the outside world. I have not been able to locate a retailer of 20 pin DIL plugs, but a 14 or 16 pin plug is often sufficient to make connections to the terminals that are of interest. If not, two 14 pin plugs carefully cut down to 10 ways each can be used. Connection details for the MTX user port are given in Figure 2(d).

The obvious difference from the electrical point of view between this port and the ones described previously is that the MTX user port has separate input and output lines, rather than a single set of eight dual purpose lines. As one would expect, POT0 to POT7 are the outputs, and PIN0 to PIN7 are the inputs. This arrangement is potentially more versatile than having eight dual purpose lines, but it is not necessarily so as the MTX user port lacks some of the additional lines found on the other machines discussed so far, and this can be a something of a drawback in some applications.

Apart from hardware differences there is also a marked difference from the software point of view. The MTX computers are Z80 based, whereas the Commodore and BBC machines use a 6502 microprocessor (or to be more accurate, the very similar 6510 in the case of the Commodore 64). With the 6502, input/output devices are memory mapped, and can be written to or read from using PEEK and POKE, just as if they were ordinary memory addresses. The Z80 microprocessor has separate memory and input/output maps, and whether using machine code or BASIC separate instructions are required for controlling each type of circuit. With the MTX computers the BASIC OUT instruction enables data to be written to output circuits, and the INP function permits input devices to be read. Whether reading or writing to the user port, it is at address 7 (i.e. OUT 7,X to write value X to the output lines, and PRINT INP(7) to read the input lines). Note that the eight output lines are three state types, and that OSTB (output strobe) must be connected to the 0 volt terminal in order to take the outputs into the active state.

This brief description of the user ports of four computers should give you a general idea of how parallel ports are used. Whatever computer you intend to have as the control centre for your electronic music system it is important to learn as much as possible about it. Not just the subject of interfacing it to external circuits, but the software aspect as well, preferably including machine code programming. It would be fair to say that the greater your understanding of the computer the more you will be able to get it to do, and the better it will be able to perform those functions. We will leave the subject of computer ports for the time being, but later in this chapter we will deal with methods of interfacing to computers without a user port or an add-on parallel port.

**CV Interface**
Having covered the problem of getting digital data into or out of a computer, we now come to the problem of converting digital output data into analogue signals that can be used to control the CV input of a synthesiser. Good quality analogue to digital converters are quite complex devices which require some precision components if they are to function well. Fortunately, several high quality digital to analogue converter integrated circuits are readily available, and despite their fairly low cost they give excellent results. The Ferranti range of converters are the most widely available type, and it is one of this range which we will

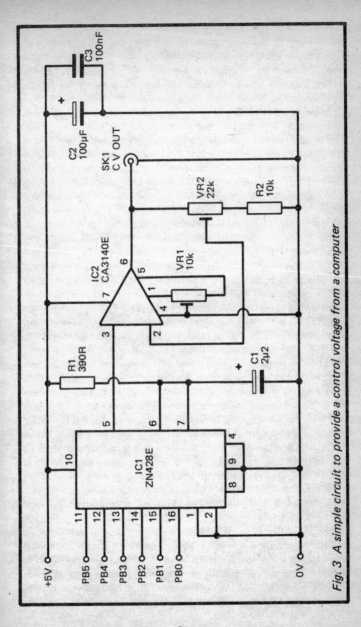

*Fig: 3  A simple circuit to provide a control voltage from a computer*

consider here. The device in question is the ZN428E, and this is used in the CV interface circuit shown in Figure 3.

IC1 is the ZN428E converter chip, and this is a standard R-2R type of converter. It consists basically of a precision reference voltage source driving a complex resistor network, with the output voltage being tapped off from the resistor network via eight electronic switches. This is in fact analagous to the keyboard arrangement of Figure 1, but whereas the keyboard circuit has one switch per note, in this case just eight switches enable up to 255 different notes to be obtained. This is, of course, achieved by selecting most notes by closing more than one switch. It is for this reason that a much more complex resistor network (known as an R-2R network) is required, and a simple attenuator of the type shown in Figure 1 will not suffice. The network is known as an R-2R type merely because it uses only two resistor values, with the higher value components being exactly twice the value of the lower value components.

It was stated above that up to 255 different notes are available, but this is an impractically wide range, and here the two least significant inputs of IC1 are simply tied to earth. This gives a 6 bit input and a range of 63 notes, or just over five octaves in other words. This is actually a greater range than most synthesisers can provide from the keyboard, but most instruments will provide the full five octaves or so when utilized with an external CV source.

IC1 has separate analogue and digital ground terminals, and these do not have to be at precisely the same voltage. However, in this case they are both simply connected to earth and do operate at the same potential. The built-in voltage reference of IC1 is a 2.55 volt type, and it requires discrete components C1 and R1 in order to function properly. The full scale output voltage is equal to the 2.55 volt reference potential, and therefore increments in units of 10 millivolts (0.01 volts). As we are not using the two least significant inputs in this circuit the resolution is reduced to nominal 40 millivolt steps. This is slightly under half the required increment, but the amplifier based on IC2 provides the required voltage boost.

The amplifier is an operational amplifier non-inverting mode circuit. Normally a −5 volt supply is needed for an operational amplifier in order to permit it to provide output voltages down to the 0 volt supply rail. This is not necessary here as the CA3140E specified for IC2 has an output stage that can provide output voltages right down to the 0 volt supply rail. In practice, whether or not a negative supply is used, there are offset errors that produce poor accuracy at low output voltages. VR1 is an offset null control that can be used to trim out these errors. VR2 is a voltage gain control, and it is adjusted to give correct scaling from the circuit. IC2 provides a fairly low output impedance and it should be able to drive any CV input without any loading problems becoming evident.

In Figure 3 it has been assumed that the unit will be driven from a the user port of a VIC-20, CBM 64, or BBC model B computer, and the connections to the interface have accordingly been marked "PB0", "PB1", etc. However, the unit can be driven from the six least significant outputs of any normal user or parallel port (POT0 to POT5 of an MTX computer's user port for example). It is not essential to use the six least significant bits, or even six consecutive bits, but it is advisable to do so as this helps to keep the software as straightforward as possible.

*CV Generator Components (Full Version) (Figs. 3, 4, & 5)*

*Resistors* all ¼ watt 5%

| | |
|---|---|
| R1 | 390R |
| R2,3 | 10k (2 off) |
| R4 | 100k |
| R5 | 1M |
| R6 | 22k |
| VR1 | 10k preset |
| VR2 | 22k preset |
| VR3 | 2M2 lin |

*Capacitors*

| | |
|---|---|
| C1 | 2µ2 63V electrolytic |
| C2 | 100µF 10V electrolytic |
| C3 | 100nF ceramic |
| C4 | 15nF polyester |
| C5,6 | 470µF 16V electrolytic (2 off) |
| C7,8 | 220µF 16V electrolytic (2 off) |
| C9 | 330nF carbonate |

*Semiconductors*

| | |
|---|---|
| IC1 | ZN428E |
| IC2 | CA3140E |
| IC3 | NE555 |

IC4          4001BE
D1,2,3,4     1N4002 (4 off)


*Miscellaneous*
SK1          Standard jack socket
16 pin DIL IC holder
14 pin DIL IC holder
Two 8 pin DIL IC holders
Case, circuit board, wire, etc.


**Voltage Step-Up**
There is a slight flaw in the basic circuit of Figure 3 in that it can
not provide the full 63 note range. Five plus octaves at 1 volt per
octave clearly needs an output voltage of over 5 volts, which can
not be achieved with a 5 volt supply. IC2's output stage will only
give a maximum output voltage of around 3 volts or so with a 5 volt
positive supply. The range of about 3 octaves that this provides
might be adequate for your needs, or you might prefer to use a
higher positive supply potential for IC2 and obtain the full range
of notes. If the computer you are using can provide a supply
voltage of about +9 to +15 volts then this can be connected to pin
7 of IC2 instead of connecting it to the 5 volt rail. Several
computers can provide a suitable voltage rail, the +12 volts
available from the MTX expansion port and the BBC computer's
power port being two examples.

   If +5 volts is the only available supply voltage it is still possible
to obtain the full frequency range, and all that is required is a
simple supply step-up circuit to provide around +8 volts from the
5 volt supply. A suitable circuit is shown in Figure 4.

   This uses the well known 555 timer integrated circuit in the
astable (oscillator) mode with an operating frequency of a few
hundred Hertz. R3, R4, and C4 are the timing components, and
these give an output that is virtually a squarewave with a 1 to 1
mark space ratio. C5, D1, D2, and C7 form a rectifier and
smoothing circuit which generates a DC potential of around 3 or 4
volts. The voltage generated by this circuit is somewhat less than
the 5 volt supply voltage due to losses through the rectifiers and
the output stage of IC3. This voltage is effectively connected in
series with the 5 volt supply, giving about 8 volts or so across C7.
C6, D3, D4, and C8 form another rectifier and smoothing circuit,
and the output of this circuit is connected in series with the
potential across C8. This gives around 12 volts across C8, and it is

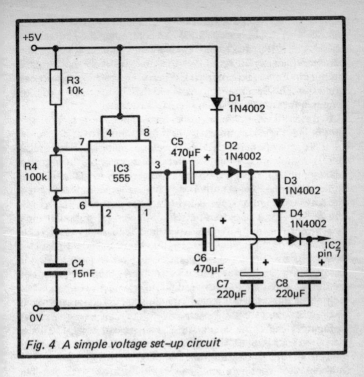

*Fig. 4 A simple voltage set-up circuit*

this voltage that is used to power IC2. Under load the voltage across C8 falls substantially, but this still leaves a supply potential of about 8 volts for IC2, and this is adequate to give the unit the full five and a bit octave range.

**Gate Signal**

In most cases the generation of the control voltage is the most difficult aspect of this type of interfacing, and the gate signal is relatively easy. If your synthesiser uses standard 5 volt logic levels there should be no difficulty if a digital output of the computer is used to directly drive the gate or trigger input of the instrument. With only six bits used to drive the digital to analogue converter this leaves two lines of an 8 bit port free, and either of these can be used to provide the gate output signal.

If the synthesiser has a trigger input the length of the trigger pulse is unlikely to be critical, but a minimum figure of around 2 milliseconds would be typical. When controlling the gate output line from BASIC, due to the relatively slow running speed of this computer language it is unlikely that an excessively short trigger output pulse could be generated. When using machine code things are different, and a timing loop would then be needed in order to lengthen the output pulses to suitable durations.

If the synthesiser has a proper gate input the length of the output pulse is more important, as it must simulate the operation of a key. With many ADSR envelope shapes a fixed pulse duration of around 10 milliseconds will suffice, but in order to make optimum use of the system it is necessary to make the gate time programmable. Another, and quite simple approach from the software point of view, is to use a pulse generator to provide the gate pulses. The output pulse duration of the computer then becomes irrelevant, with gate pulse time being set by means of a control on the pulse generator circuit. You can then adjust this control to give the envelope shape and effect you want without complicating the software with an extra timing loop. This does not permit the gate time to be altered during a sequence of notes, but in practice this is not often of great importance, and this approach is a useful compromise.

Figure 5 shows the circuit for a gate pulse generator. This is based on a CMOS 4001BE quad 2 input NOR gate (IC4). IC4a and IC4b are connected in a standard CMOS monostable multivibrator configuration. This circuit is a non-retriggerable type. In other words, if the input pulse is longer than the required output pulse duration the circuit will function properly, and there will not be any problems with multiple triggering or stretching of the output pulse. The pulse duration is controlled by the values of timing components VR3, R6, and C9. VR3 enables the pulse length to be adjusted over an approximate range of 5 milliseconds to 500 milliseconds (0.5 seconds).

IC4c and IC4d are used as a non-inverting buffer stage at the output of the circuit. R5 is merely a protection resistor which prevents static charges from damaging IC4 if the input is left open circuit. For the benefit of those who are unfamiliar with CMOS devices it should perhaps be explained that they are vulnerable to damage by high static voltages which are often present in modern environments. Devices of this type are normally supplied in some form of antistatic packaging, such as conductive foam, and they should be left in this packaging until it is time for them to be fitted

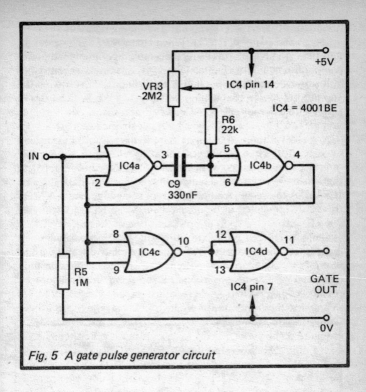

*Fig. 5 A gate pulse generator circuit*

onto the component board. They should always be fitted in integrated circuit holders, and they should be left until all the other components have been fitted in place and all the wiring has been completed. They should then be plugged in place using a minimal amount of handling. Incidentally, the CA3140E device used in the CV interface circuit has a PMOS input stage, and consequently it also requires these handling precautions.

### Gate Levels

If you have a synthesiser which does not require standard 5 volt logic levels it may be a little difficult to interface it satisfactorily to a computer, although there is nothing in theory to prevent 5 volt logic levels being converted to any desired signal levels. Some synthesisers that require 0 to +15 volt gate signal levels will just about function using standard 5 volt signals, but not all synthesisers will do so. It is not difficult to provide a voltage boost, and this can be achieved using the simple operational amplifier comparator circuit of Figure 6. However, this circuit requires a 15 volt supply, and it is unlikely that this will be available from the computer. Either a 15 volt battery supply such as a 6 volt battery in series with a 9 volt type could be used, or a mains power supply unit for the booster would have to be constructed.

Not all synthesisers require a gate voltage at all, but instead need a short circuit to earth to produce triggering. A relay interface could be used in these cases, but the considerably less than instant operation of a relay could produce unreliable results. It is better to use an electonic switch of some kind, and a VMOS transistor connected in the manner shown in Figure 7 will give good results.

Synthesisers that require negative gate or trigger voltages are quite rare, which is fortunate as these are relatively awkward to interface to a standard logic output. As these are uncommon and I have had no experience at interfacing them they will not be considered further here.

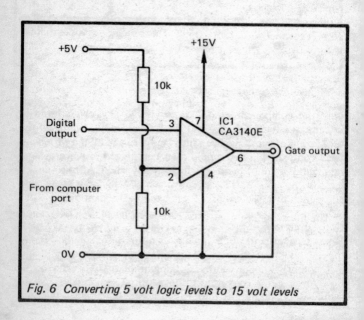

Fig. 6 Converting 5 volt logic levels to 15 volt levels

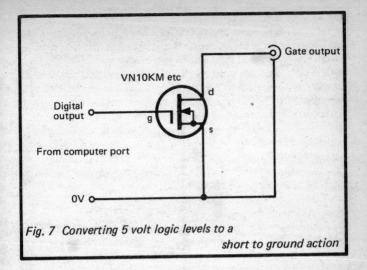

*Fig. 7 Converting 5 volt logic levels to a*
*short to ground action*

**Alternative Ports**

So far we have only considered interfacing via a user port or an add-on parallel port of some kind. There are alternatives that are worthy of brief consideration here, although in the main, it is probably best for only the more experienced constructors to attempt these methods of interfacing.

Many home computers have an eight bit output port in the form of a parallel printer port or joystick ports. If we take printer ports first, the Amstrad CPC464 computer is a good example. This has the printer port connections detailed in Figure 8. To make connections to this port a 2 by 17 way 0.1 inch pitch female edge connector is required. It may not be possible to obtain an edge connector having the correct number of ways, but with care it is possible to cut down a larger connector to the correct size using a hacksaw.

The lines that are of interest here are D0 to D6, which can be used as seven latching outputs. D0 to D5 would be used to drive the digital to analogue converter with D6 providing the gate or trigger signal. Most BASICs provide instructions which enable data to be written to the printer port one byte at a time, but in practice it is often more convenient to write data direct to the hardware that provides the printer port. In this case the data lines

17

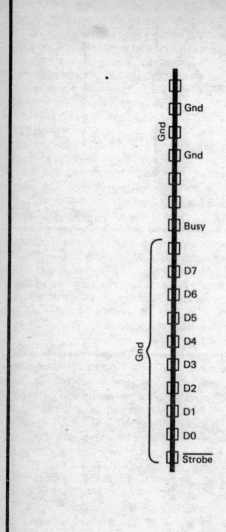

Fig. 8 Connection details for the Amstrad CPC464 computer

of the printer port are provided by a device which is at address
&EF00. Therefore, OUT &EF00,X will write value X to the
interface. There is no +5 volt supply line on the printer port, but a
5 volt supply can be obtained from the expansion port.

This system will work perfectly well with most printer ports, but
it is only fair to point out that there are one or two exceptions.
With some parallel printer ports the outputs lines are also used for
other purposes and do not latch properly. If you have some means
of monitoring the logic state of a printer output line it is quite easy
to determine whether or not it is in this catagory. If the monitored
output is static when no data is being sent to the port then the
outputs should be proper latching types and there should be no
problem in driving the interface from the port. If there is a
continuous stream of pulses on the monitored line this certainly
indicates that it is unsuitable for the present application. The only
parallel printer port of this type that I have ever encountered is the
one on the Oric 1 computer, but there may well be others.

The Atari 400, 600XL, 800, and 800XL computers have
joystick ports that can be used to provide digital outputs. The two
joystick ports each provide four lines (on the Atari 400 and 800
computers, which have four joystick ports, use ports 1 and 2).
Figure 9 gives connection details for the two joystick ports, which
conveniently provide a 5 volt supply output as well.

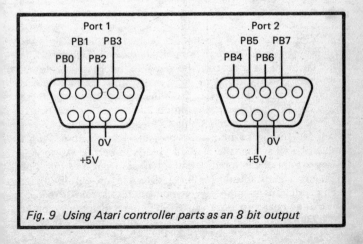

*Fig. 9  Using Atari controller parts as an 8 bit output*

The eight data lines normally function as inputs which read switches in each joystick, but the following software routine sets them to the output mode.

POKE 54018,56
POKE 54016,255
POKE 54018,60

Data for the port is then written to address 54016 using the POKE instruction (e.g. POKE 54016,0 would set PB0 to PB7 all low).

### Direct Bus Interfacing

Most computers have a general purpose expansion port which permits direct access to the address, data, and control buses of the computer, plus a number of other useful lines in most cases. In fact with some computers this is the only port available for general purpose expansion, and the one which has to be used in the present application. In most cases it is not difficult to interface devices to the expansion port, and in some cases it is a little more difficult than utilizing a proper user port. However, it has a couple of significant drawbacks in that more technical knowledge is required in order to undertake this type of interfacing successfully, and if a mistake is made there is a risk of damaging some expensive hardware in the computer. This risk is admittedly not a great one, and most logic devices are not easily damaged by such things as accidental short circuits on their outputs, but this type of interfacing is certainly not one that could be recommended for beginners.

The Sinclair ZX Spectrum has a fairly typical Z80 style expansion bus, and details of this port are shown in Figure 10. The data lines D0 to D7 carry the data for internal or external hardware, and the problem is to extract just the data that is required for the CV interface from the mass of signals on these lines. This is done by checking various other lines for a particular set of logic levels, a combination of logic levels that only occur when data for the CV interface is present on the data bus. With a standard Z80 system the method used is to decode A0 to A7, giving a total of 256 input/output addresses from 0 to 255. The eight most significant address lines (A8 to A15) are only used with memory devices, giving 65536 memory addresses from 0 to 65535. So that the microprocessor can select either a memory circuit or an input/output device it has two control lines, MEMRQ

| | |
|---|---|
| A11 | |
| A9 | A10 |
| $\overline{\text{BUSACK}}$ | A8 |
| $\overline{\text{ROMCS}}$ | $\overline{\text{RFSH}}$ |
| A4 | $\overline{\text{M1}}$ |
| A5 | −12V |
| A6 | +12V |
| A7 | $\overline{\text{WAIT}}$ |
| $\overline{\text{RST}}$ | −5V |
| $\overline{\text{BUSRQ}}$ | $\overline{\text{WR}}$ |
| U | $\overline{\text{RD}}$ |
| V | $\overline{\text{IORQ}}$ |
| Y | $\overline{\text{MEMRQ}}$ |
| VIDEO | $\overline{\text{HALT}}$ |
| 0V | $\overline{\text{MM1}}$ |
| $\overline{\text{IORQGE}}$ | $\overline{\text{INT}}$ |
| A3 | D4 |
| A2 | D3 |
| A1 | D5 |
| A0 | D6 |
| Clock | D2 |
| 0V | D1 |
| 0V | D0 |
| | |
| 9V | |
| 5V | D7 |
| A12 | A13 |
| A14 | A15 |

*Fig. 10 The expansion bus connections of the Sinclair ZX Spectrum computer*

(memory request) and IORQ (input/output request). The appropriate one of these is set low, depending on which type of circuit the microprocessor is trying to access. The CV interface must, therefore, only be activated when IORQ goes low and the appropriate combination of address line states is present.

Not all Z80 based computers adopt this standard method, and the Sinclair ZX Spectrum is an example of one which does not. The Spectrum uses all sixteen address lines for input/output addressing, but in a simplified form that gives a relatively small number of usable input/output addresses. The basic technique is to have input/output devices activated by taking one of the address lines low, and A5 is available for user add-ons. Extracting data is therefore a matter of latching data from the data bus when A5 and IORQ are low. This is achieved by writing data to input/output address 65503, and Sinclair BASIC includes the OUT instruction. Due to the adoption of this very basic method of address decoding there are in fact a great many addresses that could be used, but 65503 is the only safe one to use as it leaves all the address lines apart from A5 high, and avoids unwanted operations of internal hardware.

Interfacing the CV generator to a data bus is made very much easier by the inclusion of an 8 bit data latch at the input of ZN428E converter. If the ZN428E is fed from latching outputs the built-in latch is obviously unnecessary, and it is simply set to the "transparent" mode by taking the control input at pin 4 permanently low (as in the original circuit of Figure 3). If the device is fed from the data bus the control input must be fed from the address decoder. It is normally held in the high state and is pulsed low when the appropriate states are detected on the address and control buses. Figure 11 shows the circuit diagram of a simple address decoder for the Spectrum computer. This also includes a latching digital output to drive the gate input of the synthesiser.

The address decoding is provided by IC5 which is a 2 input OR gate. This gives a high output state if either input or if both inputs are in the high state. Looking at things in another way, it provides a low output only if both inputs are low. This gives the required action, with a low pulse being supplied to the control input of IC1 when A5 and IORQ go low simultaneously. There are three more OR gates in IC5, but these are not required here and are simply ignored.

IC6 is a 74LS74 dual D type flip/flop, but in this circuit only one section of the device is used, and this acts as a data latch. It latches

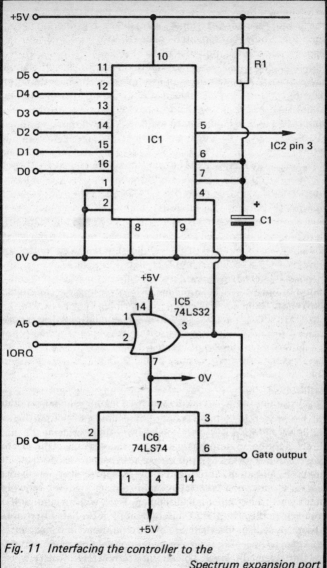

*Fig. 11 Interfacing the controller to the*

*Spectrum expansion port*

23

the data on line D6 using the same address decoder as the digital to analogue converter.

The unit can be interfaced to a computer based on the 6502 or a 6502 bus compatible microprocessor such as the 6809, but the address decoder would need to be completely different to the simple type in the circuit of Figure 11. Normally all sixteen address lines (or the vast majority of them anyway) must be decoded in order to place the add-on port at the correct address, or in a small block of addresses. Many 6502 based computers give some assistance in the form of a ready decoded output or outputs. For instance, on the 1MHz bus of the BBC model B computer there are two decoded address lines, NPGFC and NPGFD. The former goes low if any address in the range &FD00 to &FDFF is accessed, while the former pulses low if any address from &FD00 to &FDFF is accessed. One of these lines could therefore be used to provide the control pulse for IC1 and IC6.

If no facility of this type exists, then there is no alternative to designing a decoder for virtually the full address bus. Things are similar for a computer that uses the standard Z80 system of interfacing, but with the eight least significant bits of the address bus plus IORQ having to be decoded. This is something that could only be undertaken by someone with a reasonable amount of experience at logic circuit design, and might not be worth the effort. If you are interested in computer control of electronic instruments it is definitely advisable to obtain a co-operative computer rather than waist time struggling to use one that is ill-suited to the task.

## Adjustment

Once you have reached the stage where the unit is connected to the computer a certain amount of testing and setting up is necessary before it is ready for use. If you are interfacing the unit direct to the computer's buses it is important to connect the unit to the computer prior to switching on. Apart from the risk of damaging either the interface or the computer, you are almost certain to crash the computer if you connect a circuit onto the buses while the computer is turned on. Even with an add-on that connects to the user port of the computer it is probably advisable to connect it prior to switch-on. There is one point that is certainly not open to question; if the computer does not provide the usual start-up screen display and behave in a completely normal fashion after switch-on, switch off immediately and recheck all the wiring.

Assuming there are no problems, connect the CV output of the interface to the CV input of the synthesiser, and the gate output to the synthesiser's gate or trigger input. This will probably require standard jack leads, but some synthesisers may require a different type of plug. Connecting the unit to the synthesiser does not necessarily automatically switch the synthesiser to the mode where it can be externally controlled, and it will probably be necesssary to do this manually in some way. If you are in any doubt about this you should consult the synthesiser's manual which should give details of how to set up the instrument for external control.

It will be assumed here that the gate/trigger signal is derived from bit 6 of the data bus. If a value of 89 is written to the interface this will set the gate output line high and write a value of 25 to the digital to analogue conveter. This corresponds to a note two full octaves up from the lowest note of the keyboard, and VR2 should be adjusted to obtain a note that is the same as that obtained when this key is operated. If the synthesiser has a gate input the instrument should provide an output signal all the time that the gate input is held in the high state, provided the sustain control is set at a reasonably high level that is. With a trigger input things are a little more difficult. The envelope shaper should be set for the maximum decay time and a value of 89 must be repeatedly written to the controller in order to maintain an output so that VR2 can be adjusted. A simple loop program can be used to repeatedly output this value.

With a value of 65 written to the interface the gate is still held "open", and the value written to the digital to analogue converter is 1. The note obtained should be equal to that produced when the lowest note of the keyboard is operated, but in practice VR1 must be adjusted to give precisely the right note. Incidentally, it is 1 and not 0 that gives the lowest note, and 0 is not a valid converter value in this application.

This whole procedure should be repeated a few times until no further improvement can be attained, with the synthesiser tracking perfectly over the two octave range. As explained earlier, even if the synthesiser keyboard only gives a range of about two octaves, provided IC2 has an adequate supply voltage you will almost certainly be able to obtain satisfactory results over the five-plus octave range when using the interface.

## Software

The software can consist of anything from a very simple routine consisting of a few lines of BASIC to a sophisticated composer style program complete with graphics to provide a musical stave, etc. For most purposes a simple routine will suffice, although a more sophisticated program is preferable if you intend to program long sequences of notes. The maximum number of notes that can be handled depends on factors such as the amount of RAM your computer has available for data and program storage, and the size of the sequencer program. A typical home computer these days would have around 30k or more of available RAM, and even if several k are required for the sequencer program this still leaves sufficient RAM to accommodate at least a few thousand notes. Even something like an unexpanded ZX81 with its 1k of RAM can provide sequences a few dozen notes long, which is adequate for many purposes.

The basic sequence of events that the software must provide, after any required setting up of the output port, is to set the gate output high and output the first note value. If the gate signal is provided by bit 6 of the output port, the number written to the output port is 64 plus the required note value. The gate output must then be set low again. If you are using the unit with a synthesiser which has a trigger input, or you are using the pulse generator circuit described earlier, the gate output can be set low immediately. This is achieved by writing the note value to the interface. If the computer is providing a true gate pulse without the aid of the pulse generator there are two options. Either a programmable but fixed gate pulse duration can be used, so that the required gate time is set at the beginning of the program and is then used for every note, or the time can be made programmable for every note. This second method obviously gives maximum flexibility, but it can become a little tedious when programming long sequences.

Finally, a delay must be provided to hold off the next note for the appropriate interval. A fixed note duration is rather limited in scope, and this delay should be individually programmable for each note. This sequence of events is then repeated for each note. If continuous looping of the sequence is required this just requires a single line of BASIC to loop the program back to the beginning again.

It is obviously not practical to provide sophisticated software here for a wide range of computers, or even for a few computers for that matter. However, the simple program that is shown uses common BASIC words and will operate with most computers, and it demonstrates the basic way in which the program must function. Anyone who is reasonably literate in BASIC should have little difficulty in adding refinements to this basic routine.

```
10 READ NV,D
20 IF NV = 0 THEN STOP
30 POKE 37136,(NV+64)
40 POKE 37136,NV
50 FOR L = 1 TO D:NEXT
60 GOTO 10
70 DATA NV,D,NV,D,NV,D,....0,0
```

Line 10 READs the first note value and duration value from the DATA statement at line 70. The required sequence of note values and duration values are stored in pairs in the DATA statement, with the note value always being placed ahead of its corresponding duration value. If the sequence of notes is quite long it is advisable to spread the values over a number of DATA statements as this helps to keep things more manageable. With most versions of BASIC there is a limit to the line length, and long sequences would have to be spread over several DATA statements anyway. After the final pair of values two dummy values of 0 and 0 are entered in the DATA statement. In conjunction with line 20 these bring the sequence to a proper halt rather than just letting the program crash with an out of data error message.

Line 30 writes the first note value to the converter and sets the gate output high. This program line is correct for the VIC-20 computer, but with other machines the address must be changed to the appropriate figure, and if necessary the POKE instruction must be changed to OUT (or whatever). Line 40 sets the gate output low, and it is assumed here that either the synthesiser has a trigger input or the pulse generator circuit is used to give a gate pulse of the required duration. Alternatively, a delay loop could be included in the program to set the required gate time.

The note duration is controlled by the FOR...NEXT delay loop at line 50. It is not possible to say exactly what value must be used here for a given delay time as this varies from one model of computer to another. With a slow BASIC something like 150 per second of duration is needed, whereas a fast BASIC might need a value of over 1000 per second, of duration. This is obviously something that can be discovered after a little experimentation with the system. If your computer has some form of built-in timer it might be more convenient (and accurate) if this is used to control the note duration. Line 60 simply loops the program back to line 10 where the next pair of note and duration values are read, and the process repeats itself.

**Polyphonic Sequencing**

It is quite possible to computer control either a polyphonic sequencer which has separate CV and gate inputs for each channel, or several monophonic synthesisers, or a combination of the two. One way of doing this would be to use several interfaces of the type described previously, but there are a couple of major drawbacks to this approach. One is simply the substantial number of digital outputs that would be required, with an eight bit port (albeit with only seven lines actually being utilized) per interface being needed. This might still be practical in some cases, with say a user port driving one interface, a printer port driving another, and a third being connected to an expansion port. However, even if it is possible to drive three or four interfaces from your computer, this still leaves the second drawback, which is simply the relatively high cost of doing things this way. Digital to analogue converter chips are not amongst the most expensive of integrated circuits, but they are far from being the cheapest.

The standard solution to the problem is to use one digital to analogue converter plus a multiplexer and a number of sample and hold circuits (one sample and hold per channel). This still requires a fair number of digital outputs, but far fewer than would be needed if a separate converter was to be used for each channel. It is also substantially cheaper than using a separate converter per channel. It does have the disadvantage of often being less convenient in use, although this is not always the case. The block diagram of Figure 12 outlines the way in which this system operates.

The output of the digital to analogue converter feeds into a multiplexer, which in this case is a 4 channel type, but it can have any desired number of channels. The multiplexer is really just a form of electronic switch, and it connects the input signal through to one of its output terminals. Which of the outputs receives the input signal depends on the logic levels fed to the address inputs of the multiplexer. The idea is to select channel 0 and write the

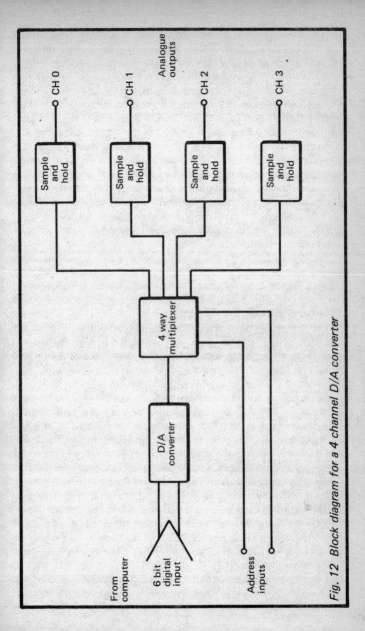

Fig. 12 Block diagram for a 4 channel D/A converter

29

required voltage to it, then select channel 1 and write the required voltage to that channel, and so on, changing the voltage on each channel as required. There is an obvious flaw in this system in that there is nothing to maintain the output of each channel at the required voltage while the converter is driving one of the other channels. This is overcome using a sample and hold circuit for each channel, and each of these circuits is a sort of analogue memory circuit which simply maintains the output voltage at the last input potential that was received. With some systems the sample and hold circuits can accurately maintain each output voltage for a period of a few seconds or more, and there is no problem in using such a system in an application such as this where each output voltage will be updated at least every two or three seconds. Some systems are less convenient, and require each channel to be updated many times per second in order to give good results.

The circuit diagram of Figure 13 is for a practical multichannel digital to analogue converter that uses the technique described above, and is well suited to use as a multichannel sequencer interface. Like the original circuit it is based on a Ferranti ZN428E converter chip.

The converter chip is not shown, but this part of the circuit is the same as for the original monophonic design. In fact the output stage is also the same, and IC2 plus its associated circuitry are exactly the same as IC2 and the surrounding circuitry in Figure 3. It is only the middle part of the circuit that is different, and here the multiplexer and the sample and hold circuits are added.

A CMOS 4051BE devices is used as the analogue multiplexer. This has an inhibit input and a bias input that can be fed with a negative bias if the device must handle signal voltages that are negative of the earth rail. Neither of these facilities are required in this application, and the relevant pins (6 and 7) are simply wired to earth. The three address inputs of IC1 are fed from three latching outputs of the computer. This gives an address range of 0 to 7, and permits up to eight channels to be controlled. In practice it is likely that no more than four channel operation will be required, and if this is the case address input 2 (pin 9 of IC1) can be connected to earth. Outputs 0 to 3 are then used, while outputs 4 to 7 become inoperative.

The sample and hold circuit for each channel really just consists of a single capacitor (C1), This rapidly charges to the output potential provided by IC1 when the appropriate channel is

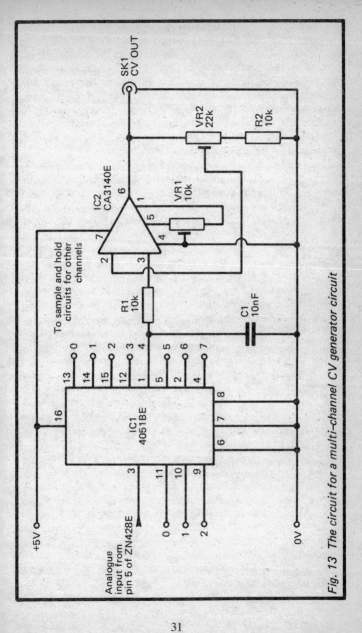

Fig. 13 The circuit for a multi-channel CV generator circuit

31

addressed, and it maintains that charge when IC1 is switched to a different channel. In fact the charge on C1 will gradually decay, since IC1 and IC2 provide a discharge path, and there will inevitably be a small amount of leakage in C1 itself. However, all these discharge paths offer a very high resistance, and there should be no significant reduction in the charge potential on C1 for several seconds. R1 is an input protection resistor for IC2.

Of course, in Figure 13 only one sample and hold circuit and one output amplifier is shown, but these circuits must be duplicated for each channel that is used.

The circuit requires more outputs than can be provided by the user port of most computers. Many computers can still drive this interface without too much difficulty. With the BBC model B computer, for instance, one way of tackling things is to drive the digital to analogue converter from the six least significant outputs of the printer port, and to drive the address inputs of IC1 from three lines of the user port. This leaves two data outputs of the printer port and five lines of the user port free for use as gate outputs. In fact full eight channel operation could be achieved by pressing handshake line CB2 of the user port into service as the eighth gate output line. But I suspect that few constructors will require the full eight channel capability of the unit.

The basic action required from the software is to output new note values at the appropriate intervals, first selecting the required channel using the lines that drive the address inputs, and then writing the value to the converter. For optimum convenience it is best to have the address inputs driven from the three least significant lines of an output port as the number then needed to select each channel is the same as its channel number. Of course, the gate signal must be provided by the computer, and the software is much more manageable if the pulse generator circuit described previously is used to provide the gate signal. It is then just a matter of outputting a new note value or a set of note values, and then setting the appropriate lines high and then immediately setting them low again. If a longer gate pulse duration is used and each channel has a different rhythm, the timing of the program would well defeat all but the most experienced programmers. With just a short gate pulse duration and the pulse generator circuit things are very much more straightforward.

An important point to bear in mind is that it takes the charge potential on the sample and hold capacitor a short time to adjust to changes in voltage. We are only talking about a typical adjustment time of around $100\mu S$, and when using BASIC the relative slowness of this language ensures that the capacitors always have time to properly adjust to new voltage levels. When using machine code it would almost certainly be necessary to provide a short delay loop to ensure the output of the converter is fed through to each sample and hold circuit for a sufficiently long time. Alternatively, C1 in each channel could be reduced in value to around 220pF, but the sample and hold circuits would then only accurately maintain output voltages for a fraction of a second, and each channel would therefore need to be updated several times per second in order to give satisfactory results. This second method might still be the easier of the two, and it is really a matter of choosing whichever system you find easier to work with. Incidentally, there is an advantage to machine code in this application, especially if you are using several channels. The speed of machine code enables the channels to be accurately synchronised, whereas with BASIC, especially one of the slower varieties, the synchronisation might be noticeably "loose".

*Multichannel CV Generator Components (Fig. 13)*

*Resistors* all ¼ watt 5%

| | |
|---|---|
| R1,2 | 10k (2 off) |
| VR1 | 10k preset |
| VR2 | 22k preset |

*Capacitor*

| | |
|---|---|
| C1 | 10nF carbonate |

*Semiconductors*

| | |
|---|---|
| IC1 | 4051BE |
| IC2 | CA3140E |

*Miscellaneous*

| | |
|---|---|
| SK1 | Standard jack socket |

16 pin DIL IC holder
8 pin DIL IC holder
Case, circuit board, wire, etc.

**Note** that additionally a ZN428E (or similar) D/A converter circuit is required, and that C1, IC2, R1, R2, VR1, and VR2 are duplicated in each channel (a maximum of eight can be used).

**Keyboard Reader**

A keyboard reader could be regarded as the opposite of a control voltage generator, and it is simply a circuit which reads the control voltage output of a synthesiser and converts it into a digital value that can be stored in a computer. In other words it is a form of analogue to digital converter rather than a digital to analogue type as used in the CV generator.

There are two main ways of using a device of this type. One is to enable note values to be entered from the synthesiser's keyboard when using a sequencer program, which is far easier for most users than typing in note values, and is my main use for this type of circuit. The second possible use, and one that many would probably consider to be the more interesting and useful, is to use the interface to record a sequence of notes, including note durations, so that the sequence can then be replayed in real-time using an interface of the type described earlier. Although systems of this type are usually called real-time recorders, they mostly have a facility to permit the playback speed to be varied over quite wide limits. This is something that can easily be achieved in a system that is based on a home-computer, and it requires software to alter the note duration values rather than some additional hardware.

The process of analogue to digital conversion is not quite as simple as digital to analogue conversion, and there are several types of A/D converter which vary considerably in operating speed, accuracy, and cost. For our present purposes we do not need a particularly fast or accurate type. A successive approximation type of converter is probably the best choice as these are widely available at reasonable cost, and generally offer a level of performance that is substantially more than adequate for this application.

This type of converter consists basically of an 8 bit register driving a digital to analogue converter, plus a high speed comparator and some control logic. Initially all the outputs of the register are set to zero, apart from the most significant bit. The output voltage of the digital to analogue converter is then compared with the input voltage, and if the former is the greater the most significant bit of the register is left at 1. If not it is set to 0. Bit 6 of the register is then set to 1, the output of the digital to analogue converter is compared with the input voltage, and bit 6 is either left at 1 or reset to 0, depending on the result of the comparison. This process is repeated for the other bits of the register, working bit by bit through to the least significant one. As this process is carried out, the number in the register gradually becomes a valid digital representation of the input voltage. It is thus the 8 bit number in the register that provides the converted digital output.

Of course, the manner in which the digital number relates to absolute voltage varies from one converter design to another. The full scale input voltage of the circuit is equal to the full scale output voltage of the D/A converter utilized in the design, and in the case of the unit featured here the full scale value is 2.55 volts. This circuit (Figure 14) is based on the Ferranti ZN449 integrated circuit, and the D/A converter featured in this device is essentially the same as the one that forms the basis of the ZN428E described earlier. The full scale value is easily altered by adding an amplifier at the analogue input to boost sensitivity, or as in this case, using an attenuator here to give reduced sensitivity.

There are various ways of interfacing the device to a computer, but for the moment we will assume that the unit is interfaced to the user port of a computer such as the BBC model B or Commodore 64, which is certainly the easiest way of doing things. Lines PB0 to PB5 are used as inputs to read the six most significant outputs of the converter chip, IC1. Like the CV generator circuit, only six bits are used, giving a range of over five octaves (which is greater than the keyboard range of any synthesisers I have encountered). The two least significant outputs of IC1 are just ignored. Incidentally, the ZN449 specified for IC1 is from a series of three devices, the others being the ZN448 and the ZN447. The ZN449 is by far the cheapest of the three devices, and is also the least accurate. However, as we only require six bit resolution in this application it still provides more than adequate accuracy, and there is no point in using one of the more expensive versions.

With a digital to analogue converter data can simply be written to the circuit at any time, and will almost instantly be converted into the required analogue value. There is a slight delay (called the "settling time") before the output takes up the correct value, but this is quite short at typically about $1\mu s$ or less. Things are less straightforward with an analogue to digital converter, and the device can not simply be read at any desired instant, with an accurate reading of the input being obtained. The converter chip first requires a signal from the computer before it will start a conversion, and then a suitable delay must be left before the conversion has been completed and an accurate representation of

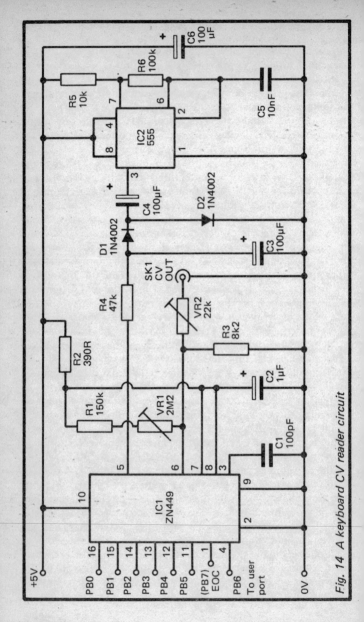

Fig. 14 A keyboard CV reader circuit

36

the input voltage becomes available from the successive approximation register.

In this circuit PB6 operates in the output mode, and it is used to provide a brief negative pulse to initiate each conversion. The time taken for each conversion is equal to nine clock cycles, and the ZN449 has an internal clock oscillator. C1 is the timing capacitor for the clock circuit, and with the specified value of 100pF a clock frequency of just under 1MHz is obtained (which is about the maximum usable clock frequency for the ZN449). This represents about $10\mu s$ per conversion. When reading the unit from BASIC each conversion will have been comfortably completed before the converter can be read since it takes around $100\mu s$ or more for each instruction to be completed even with a fast version of BASIC. When using machine code it will almost certainly be possible to take readings somewhat faster than conversions can be completed. The easiest solution to the problem is to use a short software delay to prevent premature reading of the converter. An alternative method is to monitor the "end of conversion" status output of IC1 (pin 1) using line PB7. This output goes low while a conversion is in process, and software can therefore be used to provide a hold-off and prevent the converter being read until PB7 is taken to the high state.

VR2 and R3 act as the input attentuator which reduces the sensitivity of the circuit to give a full scale input voltage of just over 5 volts. VR2 is adjusted to give precisely the correct sensitivity. IC1 does not have a built-in zero adjustment circuit, and VR1 plus R1 are used to ensure that accurate results are obtained at low input potentials.

A reference voltage source is needed for the digital to analogue converter section of IC1, and an internal source is available. This requires discrete components R2 and C2. A negative voltage is required for the comparator stage of IC1, and this could be provided by a negative supply rail of the computer where a suitable voltage source is available. However, even if a suitable supply is available it is often more convenient to use a simple negative voltage generator circuit to derive the negative bias voltage from the +5 volt supply. This is the method adopted here, and the bias generator circuit consists of 555 timer device IC2 used in the astable mode, and feeding a simple rectifier and smoothing circuit. This gives a negative bias of about $-3$ volts which is fed to IC1 via "tail" resistor R4.

*Keyboard Reader Components (Fig. 14)*

*Resistors* all ¼ watt 5%

| | |
|---|---|
| R1 | 150k |
| R2 | 390R |
| R3 | 8k2 |
| R4 | 47k |
| R5 | 10k |
| R6 | 100k |
| VR1 | 2M2 preset |
| VR2 | 22k preset |

*Capacitors*

| | |
|---|---|
| C1 | 100pF ceramic plate |
| C2 | 1μF 63V electrolytic |
| C3,4,6 | 100μF 10V electrolytic (3 off) |
| C5 | 10nF polyester |

*Semiconductors*

| | |
|---|---|
| IC1 | ZN449 |
| IC2 | 555 |
| D1,2 | 1N4002 (2 off) |

*Miscellaneous*

| | |
|---|---|
| SK1 | Standard jack socket |

18 pin DIL IC holder
8 pin DIL IC holder
Computer lead
Circuit board, case, wire, etc.

**Adjustment and Use**

In order to test the unit and set it up ready for use a simple test program is required. The one that follows is for the BBC model B computer, but there should be no difficulty in writing a version of this for any other computer.

```
10 ?&FE62=64
20 ?&FE60=64
30 ?&FE60=0
40 ?&FE60=64
50 PRINT (?&FE60 – 192)
60 GOTO 30
```

Line 10 sets up PB6 as an output but leaves the other seven lines as inputs, At line 20 PB6 is set to its quiescent state, which is high. Lines 30 and 40 produce a negative pulse on PB6 to initiate a conversion, and line 50 then reads the converter and prints the returned value on screen. PB6 will be high, and the unconnected PB7 will float to the high state, boosting the returned value by 192 (64 + 128). A value of 192 is therefore deducted from the reading at line 50 before it is printed on screen, so that it is within a range of 0 to 63. Line 60 loops the program back to line 30 where a fresh conversion is initiated, and the action of the program is to take a continuous series of readings which are displayed down the left hand side of the screen.

With SK1 connected to the CV output of the synthesiser and both preset resistors set at about half maximum value, press the highest key of the synthesiser's keyboard. VR2 is then adjusted so that the value returned on- screen is equal to the number of keys on the keyboard. Next press the lowest key of the keyboard, This should give a reading of 1, but if necessary VR1 can be adjusted to give a stable reading of 1. Repeat this whole procedure two or three times until the unit tracks accurately over the full keyboard range, giving stable readings when any key of the synthesiser is operated.

There should be no real difficulty in using the unit to supply note values for a composer style sequencer program. One important point when doing this is to make sure that a new note value is present when the value is read from the user port. One way of doing this is to have the port read when a certain key of the computer's keyboard is pressed, and it is then a matter of making sure that you operate this key after the correct synthesiser key has been operated, and not before. Automatic operation could be obtained by monitoring the gate output of the synthesiser using a digital input of the computer. Line PB7 could be used in this role, and it would then be a matter of reading the user port to determine the new note value each time a low to high transition is detected on PB7.

If the unit is used in a real-time sequencer application it is then essential to monitor the gate output of the synthesiser, since an output line of the computer must be made to simulate the gate output during playback, and it is not just a matter of sending a series of note values to the CV input at the appropriate intervals. There are two basic ways of tackling real-time sequencer software. One is to monitor the input port at regular intervals and to store the results in a block of memory. This can be very simple from the software point of view, especially if the gate input and A/D converter feed into the same bits that are used to drive the gate output and D/A converter. During playback it is then just a matter of outputing the stored values to the output port at the correct intervals. However, even if the gate input line feeds into a different bit to that used for the gate output, some simple manipulation of values is all that is needed to give correct operation of the system.

The drawback of this system, and quite a major one at that, is the need for a large amount of memory to store even quite short sequences of notes. The problem is caused by the need to sample the input port at a fairly high rate, say a hundred times a second or more for really good results. If this is not done there is a risk of short notes being missed altogether, and at best the timing of the sequence when played back might not be very accurate. With a sampling rate of one hundred per second about 1k of RAM only gives about ten seconds of recording. This system is still quite practical if you have a computer with a reasonable amount of RAM available to the user, and with about 30k of RAM a maximum recording time in the region of 5 minutes could be achieved. It is certainly the best system if you have a computer with plenty of spare RAM and are not particularly expert a writing software. With a reasonably fast BASIC, an adequate sampling rate should be achieved, and there should be no need to resort to machine code.

The problem with the system outlined above is that it is using several bytes of RAM for even quite short notes, and for long notes it may use up over a hundred bytes. The second system is much more efficient than this, and with most computers it can provide sequences many thousands of notes long, or in terms of time this works out at typically around 30 minutes or more. Even if you do not wish to store very long sequences (and probably few users would wish to do so), the ability to store several relatively short sequences in memory simultaneously can often be useful.

The basic idea of the second system is to monitor the input port, and to store fresh values only when a change is detected. In addition to fresh values, timings must also be stored. The timings are usually in the form of the time since the last change, rather than the the total time that has elapsed since the start of the sequence, as this gives smaller numbers and takes up less RAM. In fact this system need only take about 4 bytes of RAM per note.

It can be reasonably easy to implement provided the computer has a built-in timer function with a reasonable resolution (about 10ms). Without a built-in timer it could be rather difficult to implement, especially from BASIC, and the first system would then be the more practical proposition unless you are fairly expert at writing software.

### Interfacing

When deciding the best method of connecting the unit to your computer it should be borne in mind that CV reader and the CV generator do not need to be connected to the computer simultaneously. It is more convenient if they can be operated from separate ports as this will save a lot of plugging-in and unplugging. It will also avoid the risk of connecting the keyboard reader to the computer port while the latter has its lines set up as outputs to drive the CV generator (which would result in two sets of outputs being connected together). This might not damage any of the hardware, but it is better not to find out whether or not it would do so.

If you wish to directly interface the keyboard reader to the buses of the computer this will probably not be too difficult, and can be done in much the same way as interfacing the CV generator. The unit must only output data onto the data bus during the brief periods when the microprocessor tries to read the unit, and the outputs must go into a high impedance state at other times. There is no need for a separate three state buffer to be added between IC1 and the data bus as IC1 has three state outputs. These are in the inactive state with pin 2 taken high, and the outputs are made active by taking pin 2 low. Therefore, the six used outputs of IC1 can be connected directly to D0 to D6 of the data bus, and the address decoder must provide a negative pulse to pin 2 of IC1.

If we take a practical example, if the unit is interfaced to the 1MHz bus of the BBC model B computer the NPGFC output of the computer could be used to provide the enable pulse to pin 2 of IC1. The converter could then be read at any address from &FC00 to &FCFF. Some means of providing the "start conversion pulse" prior to taking each reading would be required, and the NPGFD output could be connected to pin 4 of IC1 and used for this purpose. Writing any value to an address in the range &FD00 to &FDFF would then initiate a conversion.

Using an address decoder circuit which does not decode the

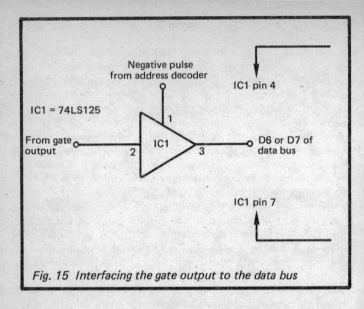

**IC1 = 74LS125**

Negative pulse from address decoder

IC1 pin 4

From gate output

IC1

D6 or D7 of data bus

IC1 pin 7

*Fig. 15 Interfacing the gate output to the data bus*

read/write line of a 6502 bus, or the RD (read) line of a Z80 bus, does involve a slight risk. The problem is that an accidental write operation to the converter would result in the microprocessor trying to write data to the outputs of the converter, which is obviously undesirable. This can be avoided by using an address decoder which processes the read/write line, which goes low during write operations and high during read operations. The Z80 has a different arrangement with separate read and write lines, with one of these going low, depending on the type of operation in progress. Read/write line decoding enables an input device and an output device to share the same address, but it is not essential to use it provided you are careful to never accidentally write data to an input device.

If direct interfacing to the computer's buses is used, it is still necessary to have a digital input to read the gate output line of the synthesiser, and this could be read by any spare digital input on the computer. However, things are generally more convenient if this input line is at the same address as the converter. A digital input can easily be provided using a three state buffer, as shown in Figure 15.

# Chapter 2

## DRUM SYNTHESISERS

Many drum synthesisers these days are fully digital. That is, they do not just use a digital circuit for triggering to generate the required rhythm pattern, but they also use digital circuits to generate the output signals. The most common form of digital signal generation is to have ROMs which contain digital recordings of real instruments, and as one would expect, this usually gives extremely good results. This type of thing can be undertaken using a suitable home computer as the basis of the system, but this is a subject which we will not cover until the next chapter.

The cost of fully digital systems is certainly falling with the passage of time, but a combination of digital control plus analogue sound generation still represents what is probably the most cost effective solution to electronic percussion synthesis. In this chapter a few simple analogue percussion generators which are suitable for digital control will be described. All the circuits are quite inexpensive but offer a useful range of sounds. Using all these circuits plus a home cumputer to control the system gives a very versatile but low cost set up, especially if you already have access to a suitable home computer and do not incur the cost of buying one specially.

### Fixed Pitch Drum

Drum synthesisers can be quite complex, but a surprisingly good effect can be obtained using an ultra-simple circuit which just consists of an audio frequency oscillator with the level of feedback adjusted to the point where it is just insufficient to sustain oscillation. If a brief pulse is applied to the input of the amplifier at the heart of the oscillator, it excites the oscillator into action, but oscillation can not be sustained and the output signal gradually dies away. This gives an output signal which consists of a tone which is initially at a high signal level, but quite rapidly at first, and then more gradually, decays to zero. In other words, it gives an output that is much the same as that obtained from a conventional drum synthesiser which uses a sinewave or triangular oscillator feeding into a VCA (voltage controlled amplifier) and envelope generator circuit.

The output from a simple "damped" oscillator circuit is more realistic than one might expect, and is probably superior to many circuits based on an oscillator plus envelope shaping circuits. However, one should bear in mind that exciting an oscillator into action is an exact electrical analogy to a mechanical drum, where striking the instrument causes the diaphragm to produce mechanical oscillations that gradually die away. It would therefore not be unreasonable to expect excellent results from synthesisers of this type.

Figure 16 shows the circuit diagram for a fixed pitch drum that uses the system outlined previously. "Fixed pitch" is not a particularly accurate term in this case as the pitch of the drum can be manually tuned over a wide frequency range. It is a fixed pitch instrument in the sense that the pitch remains constant during each burst of tone, and the frequency is not electronically modulated in disco drum fashion.

Anyone who is familiar with audio test gear will probably recognise the circuit as a Wien oscillator. One arm of the Wien network is formed by C4, R7, and VR1b, while the other arm is formed by C2, R3, and VR1a. At a certain frequency the network provides a phase shift of zero, and at the same frequency it provides its minimum level of loss (about 10dB). In order to produce oscillation at this frequency IC1 must have a closed loop gain of approximately 10dB (3 times), but in this application gain control VR2 is adjusted for slightly inadequate voltage gain. VR2 effectively operates as the decay control, since a low level of gain gives a short output signal and a well damped drum sound, whereas taking VR2 right to the verge of oscillation gives a long decay and a very resonant drum sound. VR1 enables the operating frequency to be varied over a frequency range of roughly 30Hz to 300Hz, but by making R3 and R7 somewhat lower in value the upper frequency limit can be extended if desired.

The computer provides a short pulse of around 5ms in duration which is first processed by DC blocking capacitor C5 and a simple passive lowpass filter comprised of R5 and C3. Without this filtering the pulse would break through to the output as an undesirable "click" sound, but the filtering modifies the sound to a much deeper "thud", like the initial sound of an ordinary drum. R4 couples the processed pulse to the non-inverting input of IC1 where it excites the circuit into producing a short burst of oscillation.

This circuit may seem to simple to be true, but there is a price to

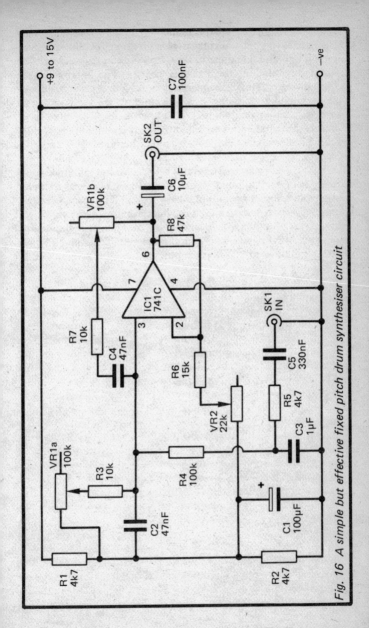

Fig. 16 A simple but effective fixed pitch drum synthesiser circuit

45

pay for this simplicity. The problem is merely that it can be difficult to set up the unit accurately to give precisely the required effect. It is likely that adjusting the frequency control will render it necessary to readjust the feedback control. The latter must be adjusted very carefully indeed in order to give the required effect, and you might consider it worthwhile to add a 1k linear potentiometer in series with VR2 to act as a "fine" feedback control. Once the unit is adjusted correctly it should produce an excellent effect that could probably not be bettered using a simple analogue circuit.

Of course, if you require several drums at different pitches it is merely necessary to build several of these circuits, and to drive them from separate outputs of the computer. If the computer has a positive supply output which provides around 9 to 15 volts and has a reasonbly low ripple and noise content, this should be adequate as the power source for the unit. Alternatively, a 9 volt battery can be used to power the unit.

*Fixed Pitch Drum Synthesiser Components (Fig. 16)*

*Resistors* all ¼ watt 5%

| | |
|---|---|
| R1,2,5 | 4k7 (3 off) |
| R3,7 | 10k (2 off) |
| R4 | 100k |
| R6 | 15k |
| R8 | 47k |
| VR1 | 100k dual gang lin |
| VR2 | 22k lin |

*Capacitors*

| | |
|---|---|
| C1 | 100$\mu$F 16V electrolytic |
| C2,4 | 47nF carbonate (2 off) |
| C3 | 1$\mu$F carbonate |
| C5 | 330nF carbonate |
| C6 | 10$\mu$F 25V electrolytic |
| C7 | 100nF ceramic |

*Semiconductor*

| | |
|---|---|
| IC1 | 741C |

*Miscellaneous*

SK1,2             Standard jack socket (2 off)
8 pin DIL IC holder
Circuit board, case, wire, etc.

**Envelope Shaper**

There is no equivalent to the method of sound generation used in the Fixed Pitch Drum Synthesiser when it comes to other types of percussive sound such as cymbals and gongs. These all require an envelope shaper to process the output of the sound generator circuit in order to give good results. Figure 17 shows the circuit diagram of an envelope shaper which is suitable for the generation of percussive sounds. The circuit is a simple attack-decay type rather than the more sophisticated ADSR (attack-decay-sustain-release) type, but for percussion sounds a simple envelope shaper of this kind is quite adequate. Suitable signal sources for use with the envelope shaper are discussed later in this chapter.

The circuit consists of two sections: one to generate a control voltage from the input pulse from the computer, and the other to give a level of gain that varies in sympathy with this voltage. Like the fixed pitch drum synthesiser, this circuit requires trigger pulses of a few milliseconds in duration.

The control voltage generator is based on IC1. IC1a operates as a low gain DC amplifier which generates an output pulse of about 9 volts in amplitude from the 5 volt input pulse. It also provides buffering. The CA3240E specified for IC1 is a device which has an output stage that can produce output voltages right down to the 0 volt supply rail, This is an essential feature for correct operation in this circuit, and one which prevents most other dual operational amplifiers from functioning properly in it. The LM358 is about the only alternative device which will act as a suitable substitute in this circuit. The input signal should ideally be provided from a MOS or CMOS logic device since these give output voltages at virtually the full supply rail potentials. In this circuit a "low" input potential of more than a few hundred millivolts could prevent the circuit from cutting off properly at the end of the envelope. The circuit did seem to operate satisfactorily when operated with some 74LS** series devices, but if necessary a CMOS buffer could be used at the input to ensure correct operation.

The output from IC1a is used to charge C1, and the low output impedance of IC1a plus the low series resistance of R4 and D1 results in C1 almost fully charging during the brief period when the output pulse is present. When IC1a's output returns to the low state D1 prevents C1 from discharging back into the output stage of IC1a, and the only significant discharge path is through R5 and VR1. This gives a much longer discharge time of around 100ms with VR1 at minimum resistance, rising to several seconds with

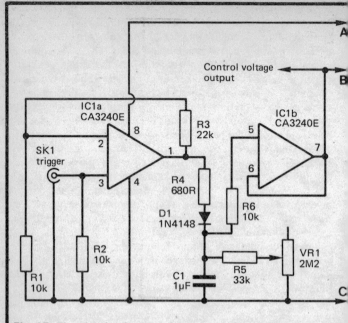

Fig. 17 The circuit of an envelope shaper for percussive sounds

VR1 at maximum resistance. C1 does not discharge in linear fashion, but exponentially. In other words, the voltage drops quite fast at first, but then gradually decays more and more slowly. This is not a disadvantage, and is in fact advantageous as it gives quite realistic percussion sounds. IC1b is just a unity gain buffer stage at the output of the control voltage generator.

The voltage controlled amplifier is a standard operation transconductance amplifier type. In this circuit IC2 is the transconductance amplifier and IC3 operates as an output buffer stage which gives the unit a low output impedance. The gain of the VCA is dependent on the bias current fed into pin 5 of IC2, and strictly speaking the circuit is a current controlled amplifier rather than a voltage controlled type. However, R9 is added in series with the amplifier bias input of IC2 so that the input current is roughly proportional to the applied voltage, and this effectively converts the circuit to the required voltage controlled operation.

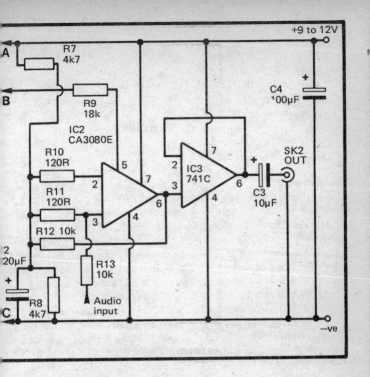

*Envelope Shaper Components (Fig. 17)*

*Resistors* all ¼ watt 5%

| | |
|---|---|
| R1,2,6,12,13 | 10k (5 off) |
| R3 | 22k |
| R4 | 680R |
| R5 | 33k |
| R7,8 | 4k7 (2 off) |
| R9 | 18k |
| R10,11 | 120R (2 off) |
| VR1 | 2M2 lin |

*Capacitors*

| | |
|---|---|
| C1 | 1$\mu$F carbonate |
| C2 | 220$\mu$F 16V electrolytic |
| C3 | 10$\mu$F 25V electrolytic |
| C4 | 100$\mu$F 16V electrolytic |

*Semiconductors*

| IC1 | CA3240E |
|-----|---------|
| IC2 | CA3080E |
| IC3 | 741C |
| D1 | 1N4148 |

*Miscellaneous*

SK1,2          Standard jack socket (2 off)

Three 8 pin DIL IC holders

Case, circuit board, wire, etc.

**Disco Drum**

The circuit of Figure 16 could be used as the signal source for the envelope shaper. Instead of setting the resonance control just below the threshold of oscillation it would be advanced just beyond this point so as to give gentle oscillation with a good quality sinewave output. This would not give a better effect than using the original method of fixed pitch drum synthesis, and it would require more components, but it would have the advantage of making the required decay time much easier to set up.

If a "disco" drum sound is required then a more complex sound source is needed. With this type of instrument the pitch of the drum is not fixed, but instead it falls as the sound decays. This requires the use of a voltage controlled oscillator (VCO) with its control input fed with the control voltage output of the envelope shaper. Figure 18 provides the circuit diagram of a suitable VCO.

The VCOs used in music circuits are almost invariably based on operational transconductance amplifiers, but this circuit is an exception as is is based on an ordinary dual operational amplifier. The circuit is virtually an ordinary triangular/squarewave oscillator of the type which uses a Miller Integrator and a Schmitt Trigger. Here IC1a operates as the integrator and IC1b provides the trigger function. Voltage control is obtained by the addition of Tr1 and its associated circuitry, and this configuration achieves good linearity over a wide sweep range.

The control voltage could be taken direct from the control voltage output of the envelope shaper, but this would restrict the unit to a very wide sweep range and would give little control over the effect obtained. Instead, R1 and R2 act as a passive mixer which combines the control voltage from the envelope shaper with an adjustable bias from VR1. VR2 enables the amount of sweep voltage added to the fixed bias to be varied over a wide

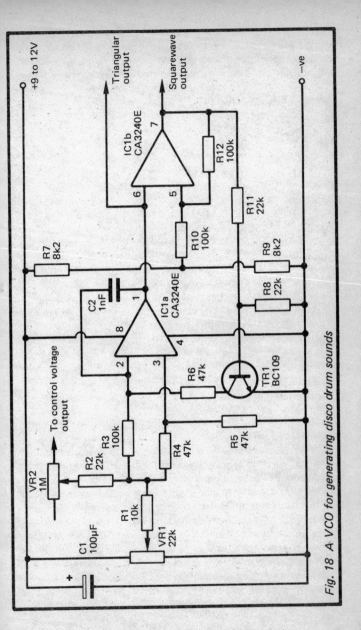

Fig. 18 A VCO for generating disco drum sounds

51

range. VR1 therefore acts as a pitch control while VR2 is the sweep width control. Together with the decay time control in the envelope generator these give considerable control over the output sound, and permit a useful range of effects to be obtained.

*VCO Components (Fig. 18)*

*Resistors* all ¼ watt 5%

| | |
|---|---|
| R1 | 10k |
| R2,8,11 | 22k (3 off) |
| R3,10,12 | 100k (3 off) |
| R4,5,6 | 47k (3 off) |
| R7,9 | 8k2 (2 off) |
| VR1 | 22k lin |
| VR2 | 1M lin |

*Capacitors*

| | |
|---|---|
| C1 | 100$\mu$F 16V electrolytic |
| C2 | 1nF carbonate |

*Semiconductors*

| | |
|---|---|
| IC1 | CA3240E |
| Tr1 | BC109 |

*Miscellaneous*
8 pin DIL IC holder,
Circuit board, wire, etc.


**Noise Based Sounds**
Many percussive sounds are noise based, with cymbals and handclaps being a couple of common examples. A really good cymbal sound requires some advanced circuitry, but some good cymbal type sounds can be achieved using a white noise source, especially if a range of filter options are available.

White noise is the familiar background "hissing" sound which we normally try to minimise in electronic circuits. There are many ways of generating this type of noise, and practically any electronic component will generate at least a small amount. In order to produce a reasonably simple noise generator circuit we require a component that will generate a fairly high noise level, and an ordinary silicon transistor is probably the best choice. In this circuit (Figure 19) Tr1 and load resistor R1 act as the noise source. R1 reverse biases the base-emitter junction of Tr1, which causes it to avalanche like a zener diode, and also like a zener diode, it generates noise spikes. In fact a low voltage zener diode could be used in place of Tr1, but this would almost certainly give a greatly reduced output signal level.

Virtually any silicon npn transistor will work to some degree in the Tr1 position, and even a pnp type will work if the connections to the base and emitter are transposed. When used with a 12 volt supply the choice of transistor should not be critical, although some devices will give more output than others. If the unit is powered from a 9 volt battery supply things are a bit more critical since the breakdown voltages of some devices are too high to permit operation below about 9 volts, and a 9 volt battery actually only supplies about 7.5 to 8 volts under load and when it is nearing exhaustion. The BC184 is one type I found to work well using a 9 volt battery supply, but probably the most practical solution is to fit a transistor socket on the component panel in place of Tr1, and then try a variety of devices from the spares box to find the one which gives the best results.

The noise output from Tr1, although relatively high, is likely to be quite low in absolute terms (typically about one or two millivolts RMS). Tr2 is therefore used as a high gain common emitter amplifier which boosts the noise signal to a more useful level.

Versatile filtering is provided by the rest of the circuit which is a state variable filter having variable resonance. This is a conventional three operational amplifier circuit having highpass, bandpass, and lowpass outputs. In this application either the bandpass or highpass output probably offers the most useful effects, but you may prefer the effects available from the lowpass output. If desired a three way switch could be added to the circuit to give switch selection of the three types of filtering.

The cutoff frequency can be varied by means of VR1 from a few hundred Hertz to the upper limits of the audio frequency range. VR2 is the "Q" or resonance control, and this enables the bandpass response to be made very narrow with high gain at the centre of the response. If highpass filtering is used the resonance control can produce a pronounced peak in the response close to the cutoff frequency, giving what is really a cross between highpass and bandpass filtering. A peak near the cutoff frequency is also obtain when the filter is operated in the lowpass mode.

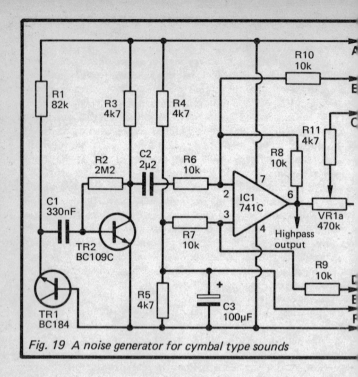

*Fig. 19 A noise generator for cymbal type sounds*

A cymbal type effect is obtained using highpass filtering, a fairly high cutoff frequency and resonance setting, and a decay time in the region of two seconds. A higher resonance setting and short decay time give a handclap type effect. However, a wide range of effects are available and it is well worthwhile spending some time experimenting with the control settings to find the effects you most like. Do not overlook some of the interesting effects that can be obtained using a low cutoff frequency also.

*Noise Generator Components (Fig. 19)*

*Resistors* all ¼ watt 5%
R1            82k
R2            2M2
R3,4,5,11,12  4k7 (5 off)

54

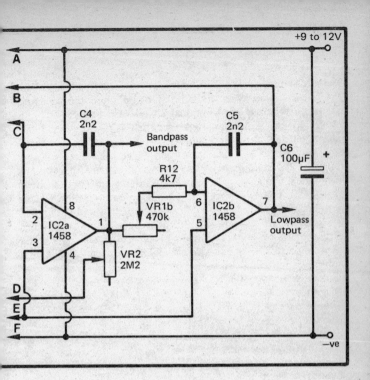

| R6,7,8,9,10 | 10k (5 off) |
| VR1 | 470k dual gang lin |
| VR2 | 2M2 lin |

*Capacitors*

| C1 | 330nF carbonate |
| C2 | $2\mu2$ carbonate or polyester |
| C3,6 | $100\mu$F 16V electrolytic (2 off) |
| C4,5 | 2n2 carbonate (2 off) |

*Semiconductors*

| Tr1 | BC184 (see text) |
| Tr2 | BC109C |
| IC1 | 741C |
| IC2 | 1458C |

*Miscellaneous*
Circuit board, wire, etc.

## Metallic Sounds

"Metallic" sounds such as bells and gongs are mostly quite complex. Whereas most musical sounds are produced by an essentially one dimensional vibrator such as a string or a tube, instruments such as gongs and bells are very much two or three dimensional. As far as the sounds produced are concerned, this results in the generation of frequency components that are not harmonically related, whereas the output from (say) a string instrument contains practically no non-harmonically related frequencies.

Electronically it is possible to produce a signal which contains strong non-harmonic components by using two oscillators and a form of mixer called a ring modulator. A ring modulator suppresses both input signals at the output, but generates strong sum and difference signals. As a simple example, assume that the two oscillators operate at 1kHz and 2.5kHz. The sum and difference frequencies are 3.5kHz (1kHz + 2,5kHz=3.5kHz) and 1.5kHz (2.5kHz−1kHz=1.5kHz) respectively. This assumes that the input signals are both pure sinewaves, and if they have another waveform that gives a complex set of input frequencies then a large range of output frequencies are generated. In practice squarewave input signals seem to give good results.

The twin oscillator plus ring modulator circuit of Figure 20 is extremely simple, but in conjunction with the envelope shaper it can provide some good metallic sounds. The two oscillators are standard CMOS astables, and their output frequencies can be adjusted over wide limits by means of VR1 and VR2. Ring modulators can be quite complex circuits, but things can be greatly simplified in this case as we are only dealing with squarewave signals. In fact the ring modulator consists of just one logic gate, IC2. There are actually three more 2 input Exclusive NOR gates in IC2, but these are not used in this circuit. The unused inputs are connected to earth to protect them against stray static voltages.

An exclusive NOR gate is an unusual and little used type of logic circuit, and one with which many readers may not be familiar. An ordinary NOR gate has an output which goes low if either input is taken high, or if both inputs are taken high. An

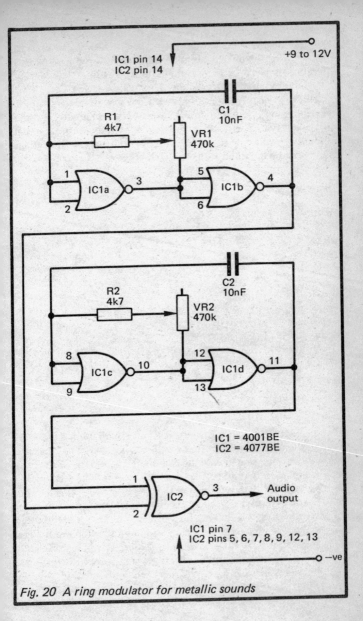

Fig. 20 A ring modulator for metallic sounds

57

exclusive NOR gate only differs from this in that the output goes high and not low if both inputs are taken high. For our present purposes this gives excellent results with strong sum and difference signals appearing at the output.

A useful range of effects can be obtained by trying VR1, VR2 and the decay control at various settings. For standard metallic (bell and gong type) sounds the two oscillators should be some musical interval apart, or just very slightly off-tune from a musical interval to give a low beat note in the output signal. Discordant sounds can be obtained with the two oscillators well off-tune.

*Ring Modulator Components (Fig. 20)*

*Resistors* all ¼ watt 5%

| | |
|---|---|
| R1,2 | 4k7 (2 off) |
| VR1,2 | 470k lin |

*Capacitors*

| | |
|---|---|
| C1,2 | 10nF polyester (2 off) |

*Semiconductors*

| | |
|---|---|
| IC1 | 4001BE |
| IC2 | 4077BE |

*Miscellaneous*
Circuit board, wire, etc.

**Software**
Three general types of software can be used with the synthesisers. The first type is a program that enables the drums to be triggered directly by operating keys of the computer's keyboard, so that you can play the drums and perfect rhythm patterns. The second type is a sort of real-time recorder so that sequences can be recorded and then played back looping continuously. The third is a composer style program that enables rhythm patterns to be entered in the form of numeric data. This third method is the most useful one for non-drummers who wish to use the system to provide a backing track while they play a synthesiser or other instrument.

Obviously the software will need to be varied to suit the particular computer you are using, but when working from BASIC it is very easy to generate the trigger pulses. First set the

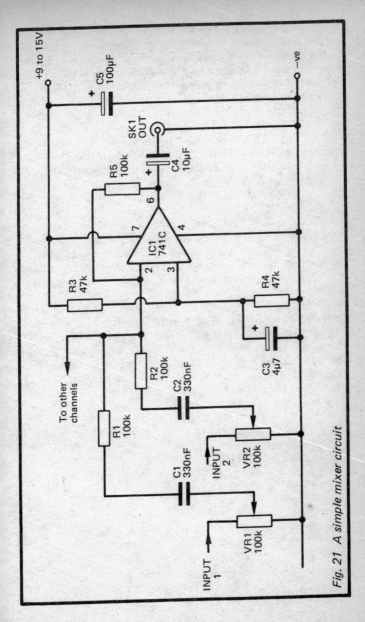

Fig. 21 A simple mixer circuit

59

user port lines as outputs (if necessary), and then simply set each output high and then immediately set it low again to generate trigger pulses. This simple demonstration program is for the Commodore 64, and it enables drums fed from lines PB0 to PB3 of the user port to be triggered by tapping keys "1" to "4" respectively.

```
5 POKE 56579,255
10 GET A$:IF A$="" THEN 10
20 IF A$="1" THEN POKE 56577,1:POKE 56577,0
30 IF A$="2" THEN POKE 56577,2:POKE 56577,0
40 IF A$="3" THEN POKE 56577,4:POKE 56577,0
50 IF A$="4" THEN POKE 56577,8:POKE 56577,0
60 GOTO 10
```

The user port lines are set up as outputs at line 5, and the keyboard is read at line 10. Lines 20 to 50 generate a pulse on the appropriate output for the key that has been operated, and then line 60 loops the program back to line 10 where the keyboard is read again.

Each drum synthesiser has a separate output socket, and an external mixer is therefore needed in order to combine the signals. Alternatively the simple summing mode mixer circuit of Figure 21 can be used to mix the signals and provide a single output. Although this circuit only has two inputs as shown in Figure 21, you can have as many inputs as you like by merely adding a potentiometer, DC blocking capacitor, and input resistor for each additional channel.

*Simple Mixer Components (Fig. 21)*

*Resistors* all ¼ watt 5%

| | |
|---|---|
| R1,2,5 | 100k (3 off) |
| R3,4 | 47k (2 off) |
| VR1,2 | 100k log (2 off) |

*Capacitors*

| | |
|---|---|
| C1,2 | 330nF carbonate (2 off) |
| C3 | 4$\mu$7 63V electrolytic |
| C4 | 10$\mu$F 25V electrolytic |
| C5 | 100$\mu$F 16V electrolytic |

*Semiconductor*
IC1                    741C

*Miscellaneous*
SK1                    Standard jack socket
Circuit board, wire, etc.

# Chapter 3

## DIGITAL SYNTHESIS

Many electronic musical instruments these days use some form of digital synthesis to generate their output signal. There are two basic ways of tackling digital synthesis, and from the hardware point of view the most simple method is to use software to generate the required waveforms. What is usually a more versatile set up in practice is to use a system of digital recording to store "real" sounds in memory in digital form, and to then play these back as and when required. This system requires more hardware though, since both recording and playback circuits are needed. This second system has another use in electronic music, and one which is at least as important as sound synthesis. It can be used as a digital delay line, and with a computer that has around 30k of memory it is possible to obtain quite long delays of around a second or so. This enables an excellent echo effect to be obtained.

One point that has to be made here is that although digital synthesis is not difficult from the hardware point of view, especially if you have a computer such as the BBC model B which is well equipped with input and output ports, the software requires a fair amount of expertise, and the hardware is of no real use without suitable software. The main problem is that BASIC is not suitable for digital synthesis of any but the most simple of audio signals as it is far too slow. It is not possible to (say) produce a 1kHz sinewave signal if the computer can only output data at a rate of a few hundred values per second. The use of machine code or assembly language is essential if acceptable results are to be achieved.

### Digital Synthesiser

We will start with a circuit that enables waveforms to be digitally synthesised from software rather than using a recording process. This is the obvious starting point as it simple, it demonstrates the basic principles involved, and it can be used as the playback circuit of a recording system, as described later. The way in which waveforms are digitally synthesised is demonstrated by the waveform diagram of Figure 22.

With a digital system it is not possible to provide signals that continuously vary in voltage in the same way as analogue signals. The computer can output a series of values, and a digital to

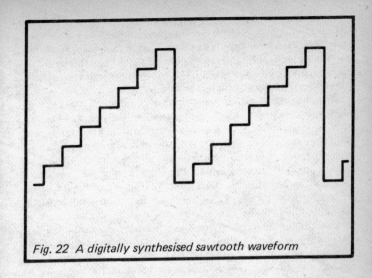

*Fig. 22 A digitally synthesised sawtooth waveform*

analogue converter then alters these to a series of voltages, but the output jumps almost instantly from one voltage to another in sympathy with the changing values received by the converter. This gives a stepped output waveform of the type shown in Figure 22, which is a digital equivalent of an analogue sawtooth waveform. In this example there are just seven steps in the waveform, which is consequently a rather poor digital representation of a sawtooth waveform. With an 8 bit system there could be up to 256 different voltage levels (including zero) which would give much better results. In fact a sawtooth waveform with 256 steps, when viewed on an oscilloscope, would almost certainly be indistinguishable from its analogue equivalent. The steps were certainly not visible on my oscilloscope when I tried this. The human ear is more discerning than the average oscilloscope, and the high frequency distortion components produced by the steps in the waveform may well be audible, but would not be of any consequence in most practical applications. In fact the level of distortion might well be lower than that of many analogue sawtooth generator circuits.

Unfortunately, it is not always possible to use the full 8 bit resolution of the system, and this is due to the relatively low maximum rate at which most home computers can output data.

Typically, around 100,000 values per second can be written to the digital to analogue converter, and although this might sound more than adequate, it must be borne in mind that complex waveforms require around 200 to 500 steps per cycle if the full resolution of the system is to be utilized. At 100,000 steps per second this gives a maximum output frequency in the range 200Hz to 500Hz.

It is possible to obtain higher output frequencies, but only by using reduced resolution, and therefore at the expense of increased distortion. This is not quite the drawback that it might at first appear to be, as although the level of distortion is increased, many of the distortion products are at frequencies above the upper limit of the audio spectrum. It is normal for a lowpass filter to be included at the output of the digital to analogue converter to attenuate the out-of-band distortion products since they could otherwise cause problems with equipment such as amplifiers or loudspeakers that are fed with the output signal. An output filter also removes any glitches on the output signal that are generated by the digital to analogue converter as it is switched from one value to another. Incidentally, the lowpass filter tends to smooth out the steps in the output waveform, and even though a signal may be made up from just a few steps, when viewed on an oscilloscope it may still be quite respectable in quality.

Figure 23 shows the circuit diagram of a digital to analogue converter plus lowpass filter suitable for digital waveform synthesis. The digital to analogue converter is based on the ZN428E device which was described earlier, and so this component and methods of interfacing it to a computer will not be described again here. In this circuit, unlike the earlier application, all eight inputs are used.

The output filter is a third order (18dB per octave) active circuit which has IC2 as the buffer amplifier. The cutoff frequency is at approximately 10kHz which gives somewhat less than the full audio bandwidth, but is high enough to give good results. This cutoff frequency and relatively fast roll-off rate ensures that minimal amounts of high frequency signal reach the output of the unit.

There are two aspects of the software to be mastered. Firstly, a section of RAM must be set aside and used to store a series of numbers that give the required waveform, or several waveforms blocks of RAM can be seeded with the numbers for several waveforms. For simple waveforms it is not too difficult to work

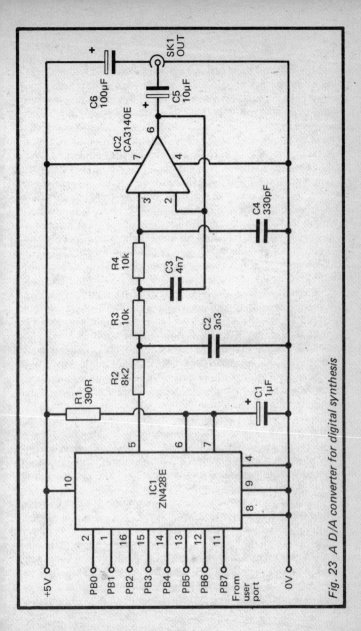

*Fig. 23  A D/A converter for digital synthesis*

65

out a suitable sequence of numbers, and a program to POKE these into the alocated section of RAM. As a few examples, a sawtooth waveform of the type shown in Figure 22 would simply require the RAM to have numbers from 0 to 255 in sequence. The reverse type of sawtooth waveform (with a downwards ramp) would require numbers from 255 to 0. A triangular waveform would need numbers from 0 to 255 and then back down to 0 again. In practice it is generally easier to have all waveforms stored in blocks of 256 bytes (pages) of RAM, and it would therefore be better to sacrifice a certain amount of resolution and use a sequence of even numbers from 0 to 254, and then back down to 0 again. Squarewave and pulse signals are relatively easy and simply require a series of 0s to set the "low" output period and 255s to set the "high" output duration. Most computers have a SIN function that can be used to generate the series of numbers to produce sinewaves of reasonable quality. Random numbers can be used to generate a noise signal.

With a block of RAM or several blocks of RAM seeded with suitable numbers, the next requirement is for a machine code routine to write these numbers, in turn, to the digital to analogue converter, and to loop continuously if a repetitive waveform is needed. This is the only part of the program that needs to be written in machine code, but it is essential for it to be in machine code (or assembly language) in order to obtain an adequate operating speed. Provided the blocks of RAM holding the sets of numbers are 256 bytes long and do not cross page boundaries there should be no difficulty in working out a suitable routine, and even a beginner at machine code should be able to tackle this without any real problems. One point to bear in mind is that interrupts should be switched off when undertaking any form of digital synthesis or recording and playback. If they are not switched off it is likely that routines such as the keyboard scan and built-in timer function will produce modulation and distortion of the output signal.

As outlined above, the machine code routine will give only one output frequency. However, the output frequency can be reduced by adding no operation instructions or timing loops to slow down the rate at which the waveforms are stepped up and down. Higher frequencies can be achieved by only using every other byte in the block of RAM, of perhaps even just one in ten or twenty if a really high output frequency is required. This gives reduced output resolution, but as explained earlier, the lower resolution should not be apparent to anyone listening to the output signal. This method of boosting the output frequency gives only quite coarse control, but if used in conjunction with no operation instructions or timing loops to slow down the output rate a wide range of frequencies can be achieved. When using only a few numbers to synthesise waveforms always try to use numbers that span a wide range, preferably something approaching the maximum usable range of 0 to 255. This gives a strong output signal at something in the region of the full 2.55 volts peak to peak output level.

*D/A Converter Components (Fig. 23)*

*Resistors* all ¼ watt 5%
| R1 | 390R |
|---|---|
| R2 | 8k2 |
| R3,4 | 10k (2 off) |

*Capacitors*
| C1 | 1µF 63V radial electrolytic |
|---|---|
| C2 | 3n3 carbonate or miniature polyester |
| C3 | 4n7 carbonate or miniature polyester |
| C4 | 330pF ceramic plate |
| C5 | 10µF 25V electrolytic |
| C6 | 100µF 10V electrolytic |

*Semiconductors*
| IC1 | *ZN428E |
|---|---|
| IC2 | CA3140E |

*Miscellaneous*
SK1                     Standard jack socket
16 pin DIL IC holder
8 pin DIL IC holder
Computer cable
Circuit board, case, wire, etc.

**Digital Recording**
In theory it is possible to synthesise quite complex waveforms and obtain practically any frequency with reasonable accuracy. It is even possible to synthesise a waveform that gives two or three output frequencies, giving a form of polyphonic output. Whether

or not it is worthwhile doing this is another matter, and it could take a lot of complex software and effort to give results that could be achieved more easily in other ways. This is really a matter of personal preference, and whether or not you find this an interesting line to persue. Ultimately though, it is highly unlikely that software to fully utilize the possibilities of the system could be produced. To get the best from a system of this type really requires some form of digital recording system so that real sounds can be recorded and fed into RAM. These can then either be played back to reproduce the original signal, or the signal can be modified in some way (altered in pitch for example).

There is more than one way in which a system of this type can be used, and it is worthwhile briefly exploring some of these here. The most simple way is to make a digital recording of a percussive instrument, and then simply play the recording back whenever that sound is required. Although most home computers will not give a recording time of more than about 1 to 2 seconds, this is obviously sufficient for some percussive instruments. A slightly different approach is to make just a brief recording (about 100ms) and continually loop this during playback to provide a constant output. A conventional envelope shaper is then used to process the sound, just as in a fully analogue sound synthesiser. In other words, a cross between conventional analogue synthesis and digital synthesis can be adopted. When using this technique it is important to loop the the recording over a section of RAM that gives start and finish values that are reasonably well matched. Otherwise there is a danger of an audible glitch each time the recording loops back to the beginning.

Another way of using the system is to have a recording made on a section of RAM, but with the program continuously looping back to the beginning of the RAM block and re-recording onto it. If the value in each byte of RAM is written to the playback circuit just before it is used for re-recording, a delay line action is obtained. Using inexpensive analogue delay line chips it is difficult to obtain delays of more than about 100ms with a reasonably wide bandwidth, but with a digital type based on a suitable home computer it is possible to obtain a delay of a second or more with a respectable bandwidth of around 10kHz. An 8 bit digital system does not give true hi-fi quality, but it gives distortion levels that stand comparison with most analogue delay line circuits. A digital delay line can be used for any of the effects in which analogue delay lines are utilized, including chorus and flanging. Probably the most popular use is to give a long echo effect though, since this is something that is beyond the capabilities of most analogue delay lines.

All that is needed to provide a digital recording system based on a home computer is a playback circuit such as the one described earlier in this chapter, and an analogue to digital converter to act as the recording circuit (or "audio digitizer" as circuits of this type are sometimes called). The audio signal must be sampled at a rate which is at least twice the maximum input frequency, and preferably at a rate of three or more times the maximum input frequency. If a lowpass filter is used at the input of the digitizer to restrict the bandwidth of the input signal to 10kHz, this enables a minimum sampling frequency of 20kHz to be used, but the sampling rate should preferably be 30kHz or more. This enables a reasonably long delay time to be obtained with most home computers, with about 20 to 30k of RAM being needed per second of delay. A typical home computer with about 30k of available RAM could therefore provide a maximum delay of around 1 to 1.5 seconds.

With a sampling rate of 20,000 to 30,000 per second the ZN449 analogue to digital converter (as used in the keyboard reader circuit described earlier) is more than adequate in this respect with its maximum sampling rate capability of over 100,000 per second. It is less than ideal in that it does not give optimum 8 bit linearity, but this can be overcome by using one of the higher quality versions. The ZN447 is the one which gives optimum performance, and is the best one to use in this application. However, the ZN449 will give reasonable performance, and is satisfactory if you do not want to incur the additional cost of the ZN447, or you could compromise between cost and performance by using the ZN448 (which is the device used in the prototype digitizer). Figure 24 shows the circuit diagram of the audio digitizer.

IC1 is used in much the same way as the converter chip in the keyboard reader circuit, but there are a few important differences that it is worth highlighting here. The most obvious one is that in this application all eight outputs of IC1 are utilized, and therefore all eight data lines of the user port are taken up by these. Some other means of driving the "start conversion" input of IC1 must be found in this case, and with the VIC-20 and BBC model B computers it is probably best to use handshake line CB2 of the user port. This can be set to operate in a mode where it produces a

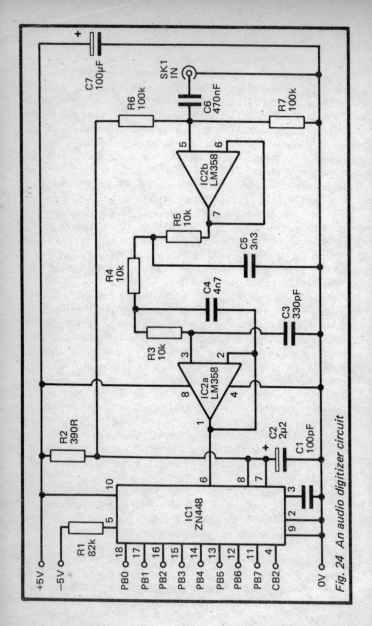

Fig. 24 An audio digitizer circuit

70

brief negative pulse each time data is written to the user port. A start conversion pulse can thus be produced by writing any value to the user port (which simply ignores the data as all its lines are set as inputs). CB2 is set to the appropriate mode by writing a value of 160 to the peripheral control register at &FE6C in the BBC model B, and 37148 in the VIC-20.

The Commodore 64 computer lacks the CB2 line on its user port, but instead has PC2. This gives a brief negative pulse after any read or write operation to the user port. This is very convenient in this application since PC2 can be used to automatically provide a start conversion pulse after each reading of the converter. Obviously not all computers have an equivalent of CB2 or PC2, but any digital output can be used to drive the start conversion input with software being used to generate the negative pulse if necessary. The method of direct interfacing to the data bus of a computer described earlier is equally suitable in this case, and the start of conversion input pulse can then be provided by an address decoder circuit. When using the system as a delay line it is obviously necessary to have the record and playback circuits connected to the computer simultaneously, and it is then not possible to operate both circuits from the user port. Where applicable, the most simple solution is to drive the playback circuit from a parallel printer port and to interface the recording circuit to the user port. Most computers do not have both types of port, and in these cases it is necessary to interface at least one of the circuits to the computer's buses.

If a spare digital input is available this can be used to monitor the "end of conversion" status output of IC1. This is not the method I would recommend though, and it is probably much easier to use a series of no operation instructions to provide a hold-off to prevent premature reading of the converter.

Tail resistor R1 is fed from a −5 volt output of the computer. The method of deriving a negative supply from the +5 volt rail which was used in the keyboard reader circuit could be utilized here, and would have to be used if the computer can not provide a suitable negative supply rail. If the computer does have a −5 volt output then it preferable to use this supply in this application as it avoids the possibility of stray coupling from the oscillator in the negative supply generator to the signal path in the recording circuit.

The filter at the input of IC1 is essentially the same as the one at the output of the playback circuit. It is preceded by a unity gain buffer stage (IC2b) which ensures that the filter is fed from a suitably low source impedance. The input of the circuit is biased by R6 and R7 from the voltage reference source of IC1. This gives a quiescent reading from IC2 of about 128, with the audio input signal varying this either side of the quiescent level. In this application a 0 volt input bias would not be suitable as it would result in the signal being halfwave rectified through the system.

An input signal level of nominally 2.55 volts peak to peak is needed to fully drive the input of the circuit, and in the interest of good performance the maximum input level should always be something approaching this figure. Otherwise the noise and distortion levels will be higher than is really necessary.

The software must obviously be designed to suit your particular application, the microprocessor used in your computer, and the address range of the usable RAM. In a simple recording application some means of hold-off is required in order to prevent the recording from being made until you are ready. Some form of automatic triggering could be used, but nothing more elaborate than operating a key of the computer's keyboard to initiate the recording need be used. A counter will be required to stop the recording when the allocated section of RAM has been filled, and this can be either a 16 bit register in the microprocessor or a couple of bytes of RAM, depending on the type of microprocessor you are using. The playback program is really just a slight variation on the recording one, with values being taken from RAM rather than written to RAM, and the generation of start conversion pulses being unnecessary. One point to watch though, is to make sure that the program runs at the same speed when recording as it does when playing back, as there will otherwise be a shift in the pitch of the output signal. Of course, it is quite in order to deliberately design things so that a shift in pitch is obtained if this is what you want. If allowed to run at the maximum possible recording speed you may find that the sampling rate is rather high, giving a relatively short recording time for the amount of RAM involved. Some no operation instructions or a short timing loop can be used to slow things down slightly if necessary, but be careful to avoid an excessively slow sampling rate as this would give a very poor quality output signal.

In a delay line application the program must be designed to output the value stored in each byte of RAM just prior to overwriting it, and the program must loop continuously. Ideally the time taken for the program to loop back to the beginning should be the same as the time taken for the program to ordinarily move on from one address to another. However, there do not seem to be any dire consequences if there is a slight discrepancy here. The length of the delay is varied by altering the size of the RAM block used. Alternatively, the size of the RAM block can be constant, and as large as possible, but the values written to the playback circuit can be taken from 1k, 2k, or whatever, behind the point where new values are written. This second method is perhaps the more elegant solution, but it is more difficult to implement, and there is a slight danger that it will run too slowly.

When using some Z80 based computers there is a slight problem due to the way in which their input/output map is arranged. Rather than using only the eight least significant address lines for input/output addresses, all sixteen are used. The Sinclair ZX Spectrum and Amstrad CPC464 computers fall into this category. This renders instructions that use the B register as a counter unusable, since the B register is required to supply the eight most significant bits of the address. Here is a basic delay line routine that will work with Z80 based computers, whichever method of input/output mapping is used.

```
        DI
        LD DE,1
        LD BC,port address
        LD HL,address of first RAM byte
        LD IY,$FFFF – size of RAM block
        LD A,(HL)
        OUT (C),A
        INI
        ADD IY,DE
        JP C,start address plus 4 (decimal)
        NOP
        NOP
        NOP
        NOP
        JP NC,start address plus 14 (decimal)
```

The first instruction disables interrupts, and as pointed out previously, a modulated audio output will result if this is not done. Next the DE register pair are loaded with a value of 1 and the BC register pair are loaded with the address of the input/output port. The HL register pair are used to provide the RAM addresses, and

73

are initially fed with the start address (the lowest address in the block of RAM). The IY register pair are used as a 16 bit counter which determines the size of the RAM block which is used for recording. The value stored here is equal to FFFF in hex (65535 in decimal) minus the number of bytes used in the RAM block. Of course, you must be careful to select an area of memory that is occupied by available RAM, remembering that a small amount of RAM is required for program storage.

The next instruction loads the accumulator with the data at the address held in the HL pair (the first address in the RAM block), and the next instruction writes the value placed in the accumulator to the output port. Although the B register is not specifically mentioned in this instruction, this is only because it would not be used to provide part of the output address with the standard system of Z80 input/output addressing. It does, nevertheless, provide the eight bit number on A8 to A15 of the address bus. The next instruction takes the value from the input port addressed by the BC pair and places it in the memory address contained in the HL pair. The HL pair are then automatically incremented by 1, but the B register is decremented by 1. Next the value of 1 in the DE pair is added to the IY pair. Apart from incrementing IY by 1, this enables the IY registers to be tested to determine whether or not they have cycled through $FFFF and back to zero (which would set the carry flag). If this has occured, the program jumps back to the point where the BC register pair are loaded with the input/output port's address, and carries on from there as before. Note that the port address must be reloaded as the INI instruction altered the contents of the B register (although this is not necessary in a computer that only uses 8 bit input/output addresses). If the carry flag is not set, first some no operation instructions are performed, which merely equalises the two loops and slows down the sampling rate to a more suitable level, and then the program loops back to the LD A,(HL) instruction. As HL was automatically incremented by the INI instruction, the program is moved on to the next byte of RAM which first has its contents written to the output port, and is then overwritten with the value from the input port.

No RET instruction is used at the end of the program since the looping process ensures that this instruction would not be reached anyway. Operating the reset button will probably be the only way of breaking out of the program. It has been assumed here that the input port has the same address as the output port, but if this is not the case it is merely necessary to add an LD BC,**** instruction between the OUT and INI instruction to switch to the correct input address.

This program serves to illustrate the basic function that the software must provide, but it is obviously only applicable to Z80 based computers and a delay line application. However, provided you understand the way in which the system must function, and you can write simple machine code or assembly language routines for your computer, there should be no real difficulty in working out simple routines to suit your application.

*Audio Digitizer Components (Fig. 24)*

*Resistors all ¼ watt 5%*

| | |
|---|---|
| R1 | 82k |
| R2 | 390R |
| R3,4,5 | 10k (3 off) |
| R6,7 | 100k (2 off) |

*Capacitors*

| | |
|---|---|
| C1 | 100pF ceramic plate |
| C2 | 2μ2 63V electrolytic |
| C3 | 330pF ceramic plate |
| C4 | 4n7 carbonate or miniature polyester |
| C5 | 3n3 carbonate or miniature polyester |
| C6 | 470nF carbonate or miniature polyester |
| C7 | 100μF 10V electrolytic |

*Semiconductors*

| | |
|---|---|
| IC1 | ZN448 |
| IC2 | LM358 |

*Miscellaneous*

| | |
|---|---|
| SK1 | Standard jack socket |

18 pin DIL IC holder
8 pin DIL IC holder
Computer lead
Circuit board, case, etc.

## Compander

Although the basic recording and playback system described here gives reasonable audio quality, one way in which it far from ideal is in terms of noise performance. The importance of the noise level depends on the application, but with a signal to noise ratio of around 46dB it would be inadequate in this respect for many applications. The situation can be greatly improved by using a compander noise reduction system, and an impressive signal to noise ratio of around 80dB can then be achieved.

A compander is really two circuits, a compressor used when recording and an expander used during playback. The compressor is a circuit which has a level of gain that varies in sympathy with the average amplitude of the input signal. The circuit is arranged so that the voltage gain reduces as the average amplitude is increased. The effect of this is to boost low level signals so that they are raised well above the noise level, but there is no boost in gain on high level signals so that they are not clipped and seriously distorted.

Compression on its own helps to make the wanted signal stand out above the background noise level, but it has the undesirable effect of distorting the dynamics of the signal, giving degrees of loudness with the signal never really becoming quiet. The expander counteracts this by providing a level of voltage gain which decreases in sympathy with decreases in the average signal amplitude. High level signals, as with the compressor circuit, are allowed to pass through with no change in amplitude, but low level signals are attenuated, thus reinstating the dynamic range of the original signal. At least, if the compressor and expander have complementary characteristics, the overall effect is to give no change in the dynamic levels.

This may seem rather pointless, but the point to note is that low level signals during playback are attenuated in order to bring them down to their original level. This attenuation also applies to any system noise, and the background "hiss" level is reduced. At high signal levels the system has little or no effect, but this does not matter as the signal will be strong enough to mask the background noise, and the low signal to noise ratio will not be evident to anyone listening to the audio output signal.

Compander systems can be quite complex, and can be very difficult to set up properly once built. Fortunately there are now special compander integrated circuits which enable a very effective system to be built at quite low cost, using very few

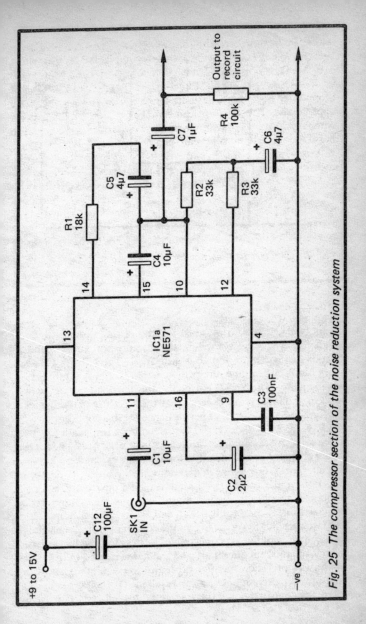

Fig. 25 The compressor section of the noise reduction system

77

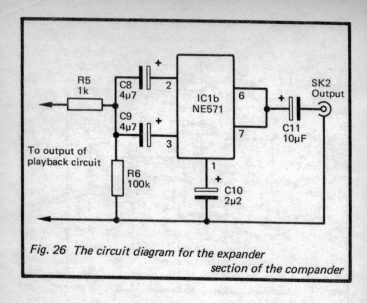

*Fig. 26 The circuit diagram for the expander*
*section of the compander*

components, and with no need for any setting up adjustments whatever. The device used in the compressor and expander circuits of Figures 25 and 26 is an NE571. The NE570 will also work in the circuit, and differs only in that it offers slightly better audio quality. The NE571 is probably the more suitable of the two devices as it is generally cheaper than the NE570, and it provides a perfectly adequate level of performance for this application.

Only one NE570 or NE571 is needed for a compander system since each device contains two identical sets of circuits, one for use in the compressor and the other for use in the expander. The basic circuit blocks are connected differently in order to give one function or the other. Each section of the device consists of a precision rectifier, voltage controlled amplifier, a reference voltage source (used for biasing), and an operational amplifier.

If we consider the operation of the compressor first, the voltage controlled amplifier is connected in the negative feedback circuit of the operational amplifier, and the latter is used in the signal path. The precision rectifier processes the output signal of the circuit, and after smoothing the resultant DC voltage is used to drive the control input of the voltage controlled amplifier. At low signal levels the output signal and control voltage are small, giving low gain from the voltage controlled amplifier. However, this gives little feedback over the operational amplifier which consequently has a high voltage gain. At higher input levels the output signal and control voltage becomes much larger, giving higher gain from the voltage controlled amplifier. This gives a large amount of feedback over the operational amplifier which accordingly has a reduced level of voltage gain, and the required compression is obtained.

The expander is somewhat more straightforward, and the voltage controlled amplifier is placed in the signal path. Actually, the operational amplifier is also placed in the main signal path, but it merely acts as a buffer amplifier at the output of the voltage controlled amplifier. The precision rectifier is fed with the input signal, and as before, its output is smoothed and used to provide the control voltage for the voltage controlled amplifier. With the precision rectifier driven by the input signal, the control voltage to the voltage controlled amplifier is proportional to the average amplitude of the input signal. The control voltage therefore increases as the input signal is increased, providing the required increase in gain and volume expansion.

The NE570 and NE571 require a minimum supply voltage of 6 volts, and will therefore not operate properly from a 5 volt computer supply. Any reasonably well smoothed supply of around +9 to +15 will give good results, and a 9 volt battery will suffice as the power source if the computer does not have a suitable power supply output.

The expander and compressor circuits have a 2:1 characteristic which, in theory, means they provide a doubling of the signal to noise ratio from around 46dB to 92dB, but in practice factors such as noise in the compressor and expander circuits have to be taken into account. This still gives the overall recording/playback system an effective signal to noise ratio of around 80dB, which is actually better than many pieces of hi-fi equipment

*Noise Reduction System Components (Figs. 25 & 26)*

*Resistors* all ¼ watt 5%

| | |
|---|---|
| R1 | 18k |
| R2,3 | 33k (2 off) |
| R4,6 | 100k (2 off) |
| R5 | 1k |

*Capacitors*

| | |
|---|---|
| C1,4,11 | 10μF 25V electrolytic (3 off) |
| C2,10 | 2μ2 63V electrolytic (2 off) |
| C3 | 100nF polyester |
| C5,6,8,9 | 4μ7 63V electrolytic (4 off) |
| C7 | 1μF 63V electrolytic |
| C12 | 100μF 16V electrolytic |

*Semiconductor*

| | |
|---|---|
| IC1 | NE571 or NE570 |

*Miscellaneous*

16 pin DIL IC holder, Input & Output Sockets
Circuit board, wire, etc.

## Mic Preamp

If you wish to use the system to record "live" sounds it is necessary to add a microphone preamplifier ahead of the recording circuit, since a microphone has an output level that is far too low to permit it to directly drive the recording circuit properly. The circuit diagram of a simple microphone preamplifier for use with a high impedance dynamic microphone, or one which has similar output characteristics (such as an electret type with a built-in step up transformer), is shown in Figure 27.

The output signal from a high impedance microphone is at most only a few millivolts RMS, and could be under a millivolt RMS. In terms of peak to peak voltage this corresponds to a signal level of as little as 2.5 millivolts, or only about one thousandth of the required drive level of 2.55 volts peak to peak. The preamplifier must therefore give a total voltage gain of about 60dB.

This design is based on a dual operational amplifier, and one section of the device (IC1a) operates as a non-inverting amplifier having a voltage gain of around 48 times (34dB). R3 sets the input impedance of the circuit at nominally 22k, which is well suited to most high impedance microphones. R1, R2, and C2 form a centre tapping on the supply lines which is used as a bias source for both sections of IC1. Incidentally, IC1 is a bifet type which has a junction fet input stage that gives a quite low noise level. It also gives excellent distortion performance. Note that as IC1 is a Jfet type and not a MOS fet device it does not require antistatic handling precautions.

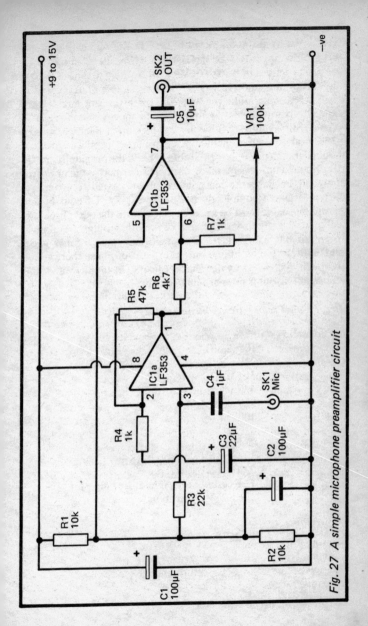

Fig. 27 A simple microphone preamplifier circuit

The second stage of IC1 operates in the inverting mode, and it is driven direct from the output of IC1a. R6, R7, and gain control VR1, are the negative feedback circuit. The voltage gain of this stage can be varied by means of VR1 from about 20 times (26dB) with VR1 at maximum resistance, down to a loss of about 14dB with VR1 at minimum resistance. This gives the circuit the required maximum overall voltage gain of approximately 60dB.

The circuit is quite sensitive to stray pick up of electrical noise, and digital systems, including computers, produce prolific amounts of such noise. It is advisable to build the preamplifier as a self contained unit in a metal case which is earthed to the negative supply rail. Probably the best power source is a small 9 volt battery which will give a completely noise-free supply. Of course, the microphone cable must be a screened lead with the outer braiding earthed to the negative supply rail of the preamplifier. Although the circuit has a high level of voltage gain plus a fairly wide bandwidth, as the input and output are out-of-phase there is not too much risk of stray feedback causing instability, and the component layout is not particularly critical.

*Microphone Preamp Components (Fig. 27)*

*Resistors* all ¼ watt 5%

| | |
|---|---|
| R1,2 | 10k (2 off) |
| R3 | 22k |
| R4,7 | 1k (2 off) |
| R5 | 47k |
| R6 | 4k7 |
| VR1 | 100k lin |

*Capacitors*

| | |
|---|---|
| C1,2 | 100$\mu$F 16V electrolytic (2 off) |
| C3 | 22$\mu$F 16V electrolytic |
| C4 | 1$\mu$F carbonate or miniature polyester |
| C5 | 10$\mu$F 25V electrolytic |

*Semiconductor*

| | |
|---|---|
| IC1 | LF353 or TL072 |

*Miscellaneous*

SK1, SK2     3.5mm jack socket (2 off)
8 pin DIL IC holder
Circuit board, metal case, etc.

## Echo

In order to obtain a repetitive echo effect it is necessary to have a mixer at the input of the digital delay line circuit. One input is fed with the input signal and the other is fed from the output of the delay line. By varying the amount of delayed signal that is mixed into the input signal the decay time of the echo effect can be altered. Be careful not to use an excessive amount of feedback as this will cause the echo signal to build up in level, rather than gradually decay, eventually giving what would really just be a noise output signal.

The mixer circuit of Figure 21 which was described earlier is suitable for this application. The input signal would be fed direct to C1 and VR1 would be omitted. The delayed signal would then be fed to input 2 of the circuit.

## Chapter 4

## MIDI INTERFACING

At the time of writing this the MIDI interface has only just started to become a standard feature of electronic instruments, but it is not really new as it has been in existence for two or three years, as have instruments that use the MIDI system. The idea of the MIDI interface is a simple, perhaps obvious one, and it is intended to enable one electronic instrument to be used to control another instrument so that the two can effectively be combined to operate as a single instrument. In fact it is quite feasable to have several instruments MIDI linked, and effectively operating as one large and sophisticated instrument.

Linking of electronic instruments has been possible in the past, but usually only in a fairly basic manner, Also, if you had instruments from a variety of manufacturers there could be difficulties in getting one instrument to control another. In some cases a special lead or a simple interface would be all that were required, but in other cases it would be impossible to provide effective links between the instruments.

MIDI, which stands for "Musical Instrument Digital Interface", is intended to enable any MIDI equipped instrument (or other device) to be connected to and used with any other item of MIDI equipment, regardless of just what the particular instruments happen to be, and which manufacturer(s) produced them. Furthermore, it is not just a very basic system which just gives gating information, or note values. It is designed to be able to communicate other information such as how hard a key is depressed on a touch sensitive keyboard. On the other hand, an instrument which only requires something fairly basic like gate pulses can still be used with a more sophisticated instrument, and it will be designed to simply ignore any information which is superfluous to its operation. It is therefore quite possible to use (say) a touch sensitive sixteen channel synthesiser with an electronic drum kit, provided both have a MIDI interface of course.

### Computer Control

Although we have so far only considered the possibility of connecting one MIDI instrument to another, what makes the MIDI interface particularly useful is the possibility of computer control. Interfacing a home computer to a MIDI instrument is not very difficult in most cases, and it can greatly increase the versatility of the instrument. In particular, there is the possibility of using (say) a polyphonic synthesiser plus a percussion synthesiser with a composer style program. Many home computers have built-in sound generators which can generate quite impressive music when used with a good composer program, but they do not compare with the results that can be obtained with synthesisers, electric pianos, and other MIDI equipped instruments that are now available. With a home computer, suitable software, and one or two MIDI equipped instruments, you have what is virtually a personal orchestra.

## Serial Data

Before considering a practical MIDI computer interface it would perhaps be as well to explain some basics of MIDI operation. One important difference between the MIDI system and any of the interfaces described in previous chapters of this book is that it is fully digital. If any analogue to digital conversion is required (and many electronic musical instruments are now fully digital) it takes place within the MIDI instrument, and is not something with which the user needs to become involved.

Another difference between the MIDI interface and those so far covered in this book is that it is a serial type. In the CV generator interface the six bits of data are written to the digital to analogue conveter simultaneously using six different lines, or in what is called "parallel" form. In a serial system the data is transmitted on just one line (plus an earth line), but this obviously precludes simultaneous transmission of all the bits. Instead they must be transmitted one at a time, and with most serial systems (including the MIDI one) the least significant one is sent first, running through in sequence to the most significant bit. This has the advantage of only needing two wires to connect one item of equipment to another, rather than about seven to nine wires (depending on the number of bits used in the system). Less obviously, with parallel data systems it is normally necessary to have screening leads, and to keep connecting leads quite short (about 2 metres or less), to prevent corruption of data due to stray coupling from one lead to another. With serial data systems quite long leads can usually be accommodated without any problems.

In the fundamental form outlined above a serial system can not operate properly, since the receiving equipment will have no way of knowing when to test the transmission line to determine the state of each bit. One way around the problem is to use a synchronous system where a third line is used to carry a clock signal or some other form of synchronisation signal to indicate the start of each data stream. Most serial systems are asynchronous though, and the MIDI system falls into this catagory. With this system there are no additional connection lines, but instead additional bits are transmitted along with the data bits. Of most importance is the "start" bit, and this indicates to the receiving equipment that it must sample the data line at regular intervals thereafter until the state of each bit has been detected. With most practical systems one or two extra bits are added onto the end of each byte, and these are called "stop" bits. These are just used as part of a simple form of error checking. Extra bits called "parity" bits are sometimes added, and these are again used as part of a simple error checking process. However, these do not apply to MIDI interfaces. Figure 28 illustrates the way in which serial data is transmitted, and this might help to clarify the system for you.

There are a number of different word formats in common use in serial systems, but for MIDI purposes 1 start bit, 8 data bits, 1 stop bit, and no parity is the one that is used. Serial data systems use a variety of baud rates, and there are several standard ones from 50 to 19200 baud. The baud rate is simply the number of bits transmitted per second if there is a continuous data stream. The MIDI system originally operated at 19200 baud, but it was criticised for being too slow (despite the fact that this is the fastest rate in common use apart from the final MIDI system). In fact a baud rate of 19200 is not quite as fast as it might at first appear, bearing in mind that ten bits must be transmitted to transfer one byte of information. This gives an absolute maximum of 1920 bytes per second, or just over 0.5ms per byte. Even taking into account that three bytes normally need to be transmitted to produce each action from the instrument, and that several channels may be controlled, it would still take just a few milliseconds to send blocks of data. Whether or not this would produce audible problems is debatable, but in the final system the baud rate was increased to 31250 baud.

The MIDI system is essentially the same as the RS232C and RS423 serial ports fitted to many home computers, but in points of detail there are problems which make it highly unlikely that a serial output from a computer could be used to drive a MIDI input. The first problem is that MIDI interfaces use standard 5

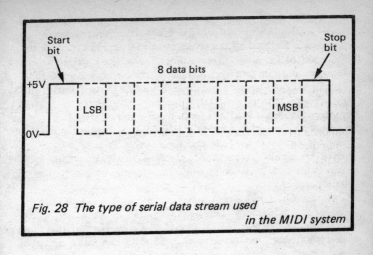

Fig. 28 *The type of serial data stream used in the MIDI system*

volt TTL levels, and normally have opto-isolator inputs to avoid problems with earth loops. RS232C ports use signal levels of nominally plus and minus 12 volts (plus and minus 5 volts in the case of the RS423). This could be overcome with suitable signal processing stages, but there is a more difficult problem with the baud rate. 31250 baud is not a standard rate, and it is not one that can be achieved with any home computer I have encountered. It might be possible to modify the serial interface to operate at the correct baud rate, but this would almost certainly render it unusable for other purposes, and would probably not be a very good idea.

As we shall see later, the integrated circuits that are intended primarily for use in RS232C and similar interfaces can be made to work perfectly well in a MIDI application, and using one of these devices it is not too difficult to add a MIDI output to most computers. Incidentally, the baud rate of 31250 baud may seem a slightly odd choice, but it is in fact a convenient one as a suitable clock frequency for the interface device can be obtained by dividing a 1MHz signal by 32, a 2MHz signal by 64, or a 4MHz signal by 128.

## Control Bytes

The MIDI hardware to provide a link between two pieces of equipment is only half the problem solved, and in order for the link to be of any practical value there has to be a standard way of interpretting data sent from one piece of equipment to another. A system of codes is used, and anyone wishing to experiment with computer control of MIDI equipment must have at least a reasonable understanding of how these codes operate.

Three bytes are needed to send each note to the synthesiser, and these provide the following functions:-

Byte 1:  Status information which indicates that the following two bytes refer to the triggering of a note, and the MIDI channel number.

Byte 2:  The note value

Byte 3:  The velocity value.

There are sixteen MIDI channels available, and these are selected using numbers from 0 to 15. This can cause confusion since you will often find references to MIDI channels being in the range 1 to 16. The difference is that the 1 to 16 range is merely used for identification purposes, whereas numbers from 0 to 15 are actually used to select these channels. Thus, if you have a synthesiser which operates on channel 12, the channel value used to direct data to it would be 11. Some instruments will only operate on one particular channel, but with most modern instruments you can set up the instrument to operate on any desired channel.

Of course, the point of having several channels is to enable several instuments to be fed from a MIDI output, with each instrument only responding to the particular data which is intended for it (and containing the right channel identification number). It is possible to have two instruments using the same channel, but only if they must both be fed with the same data. If you have a polyphonic synthesiser or other multichannel instrument it will almost certainly have a separate MIDI channel for each voice, so that each voice can be independently controlled. Incidentally, most MIDI instruments have, three MIDI sockets. These are separate input and output sockets, plus a MIDI THRU socket. The latter simply enables the data fed to the input socket to be easily tapped off and connected through to another instrument. In this way several instruments can be controlled from a single MIDI output if desired.

The velocity value only applies to touch sensitive instruments, but this byte will still be transmitted by instruments that lack this facility. They will usually transmit the maximum value of 127. It is essential that this byte is transmitted in order to maintain compatibility between MIDI instruments of various types. If some instruments were to transmit more bytes per note than others this would obviously prevent them from operating properly together. Of course, a non-touch sensitive instrument will simply discard the value in the velocity byte and can not make use of it.

If we now examine each byte in a little more detail, the header byte is divided into two 4 bit nibbles. The most significant nibble is set to 1001 to indicate that a note is to be triggered. The least significant nibble contains the channel number. Thus 10010011 would specify that a note is to be triggered (1001) on channel 4 (0011). Few computers permit numbers to be entered in binary form, and this is a rather long winded way of doing things anyway. Rationalising things, the first byte is equal to 143 plus the MIDI channel identification number (or 144 plus the true MIDI channel value).

The note value is in the range 1 to 127, and the notes are spaced a semitone apart with middle C at a value of 60. This gives a range of over ten octaves. Even if the synthesiser only has a keyboard range of four or five octaves, you will probably find that via the MIDI interface the full ten octaves or so are available, or that something approaching this full range can be achieved anyway. However, this is something that varies from one instrument to another, and a little experimentation will determine the usable range of values for a particular instrument.

A value range of 1 to 127 is also used for the velocity byte. Low numbers represent a low velocity, or a lightly struck key – high numbers represent a high velocity and heavily struck key.

So far we have considered this process as triggering a note, but what we are really doing is gating the note on. In other words we are only simulating the pressing of a key on the keyboard, and we must also release the note. This is done in much the same way as gating the note on, and it again requires three bytes. The second and third bytes are actually the same as used when activating the note, but the first byte is slightly different. The binary code in the most significant nibble is 1000, but the least significant byte is again the MIDI channel value. The decimal number used here is therefore 127 plus the MIDI channel identification number, or 128 plus the true MIDI channel value.

It is generally possible to control other parameters via a MIDI interface by using the appropriate header code and accompanying data, but the facilities available vary considerably from one instrument to another. The instrument's manual should give full details of what can be controlled via the MIDI interface, together with the appropriate control code details. It is not essential to use codes other than those outlined above, since they provide control of the important parameters, and enable multichannel touch sensitive sequencing to be achieved. Each voice can be adjusted to give the desired effect prior to starting a sequence, and it is not necessary to undertake this type of thing via the MIDI interface unless changes are required during a sequence.

## Modes

There are three common MIDI operating modes, and these were originally called "Omni", "Poly", and "Mono", but these names have now been replaced with numbers 1, 3, and 4 respectively. The most sophisticated instruments have all three modes, but the more simple types just have one or two modes. The basic idea is to choose a mode that, where necessary, effectively brings the sophisticated instrument controlling the system down to the same level as the less sophisticated one that is being controlled.

## Omni (1)

All instruments default to this mode at switch-on, and all MIDI instruments therefore have this mode. In this mode the receiving equipment will respond to note on/off information regardless of what channel it is on. Just how individual voices of a polyphonic instrument respond to received notes depends on the method of internal assignment used on the instrument concerned. The main point of this mode is that it enables a number of instruments to be controlled from one instrument (or controller), and all the instruments will play in unison.

## Poly (3)

In this mode instruments can be assigned to a certain channel, and data can therefore be directed to just one instrument even if several instruments are being fed from a single source. As for the omni mode, just how an instrument responds to each note depends on its method of internal assignment.

## Mono (4)

If an instrument has several channels, each with a different voice, by using this mode it is possible to assign each voice to a separate MIDI channel, but they must be consecutive channels. If you are using a computer to provide multipart sequencing then this is the best mode to choose, as it gives individual control over each voice. For monophonic sequencing the default (omni) mode will suffice.

There is a mode 2 incidentally, but (at the time of writing this anyway) it is exclusive to Yamaha synthesisers. It simply gets all channels of all synthesisers to play the same notes.

## MIDI Interface

A MIDI interface can be provided by virtually any of the serial interfaces that are normally used for RS232C serial ports, such as the 6850 or Z80 DART. The high baud rate is not a real problem as most serial interface devices will operate at maximum baud rates of around 250 to 500 kilobaud. Most serial interface devices are designed to connect direct to the buses of one particular microprocessor family, and could not easily be made to operate from a user port or other parallel output port. There is one type of serial interface device which is the exception to the rule, and this is the UART (universal asynchronous receiver/trasmitter) type. By using one of these it is possible to produce a MIDI interface which should operate with any computer that can provide nine digital output lines. Figure 29 gives the circuit of a "universal" MIDI interface of this type, and the unit is based on the 6402 industry standard UART.

## UART

Figure 29 includes connection details for use with the BBC model B and VIC-20 user ports. PB0 to PB7 are used to drive the eight data inputs of UART IC1, and CB2 drives the TBRL (transmitter buffer register load) input. The latter must be pulsed low in order to load the eight bits of data into the transmitter buffer register, from where they are then loaded into the transmitter register and transmitted in serial form. With the suggested method of connection CB2 would be used in the mode where it automatically provides a negative output pulse after each write operation to the user port. This is very convenient as it results in any data written to the user port being automatically transmitted from the serial output of IC1. If the interface is used with the Commodore 64 it would be possible to obtain similar results by using PC2 instead of CB2. With other computers it might be necessary to use an ordinary digital output with sofware generating the negative pulse

91

on TBRL. Another possibilty worth investigating would be to drive the circuit from a parallel printer output, with the Strobe line being used to drive TBRL. However, this would only work with a printer port that can provide full 8 bit output codes (some can only give seven bits of data, with the most significant bit always being low).

C1 and R1 provide a long reset pulse to IC1 at switch-on. IC2a is a 2 input NOR gate but it is used here as an inverter at the serial output of IC1. This is essential as the direct serial output from IC1 is of the wrong polarity, and it would have no effect if coupled to a MIDI input. IC1 has a built-in divide by 16 action at the clock input, and it therefore requires a clock frequency at 16 times the baud rate, or 500kHz in this case. The clock signal is provided by two gates of IC2 which are used in a simple crystal oscillator circuit. A 500kHz ceramic resonator is suitable as an inexpensive substitute for crystal X1 incidentally. The fourth gate of IC2 is not used in this circuit.

IC1 is capable of handling a wide range of different word formats, and five of its inputs are tied to one or other of the supply rails in order to program the required format. The method of connection shown in Figure 29 gives the correct mode with 1 start bit, 8 data bits, 1 stop bit, and no parity bit.

It should perhaps be explained that the 6402 is capable of both serial transmission and reception, but in this circuit only the transmitter section is utilized. It is unlikely that a practical application would require the computer to read data from a MIDI device and there would consequently be little point in trying to implement the receiver section.

The standard type of plug/socket used for MIDI interfaces is the 5 way (180 degree) DIN type. Figure 30 shows the correct method of connecting the output of the interface to the MIDI input of the synthesiser or other instrument.

*MIDI Interface Components (Fig. 29)*

*Resistors* all ¼ watt 5%

| | |
|---|---|
| R1 | 47k |
| R2 | 4M7 |

*Capacitors*

| | |
|---|---|
| C1 | 10$\mu$F 25V electrolytic |
| C2 | 68pF ceramic |

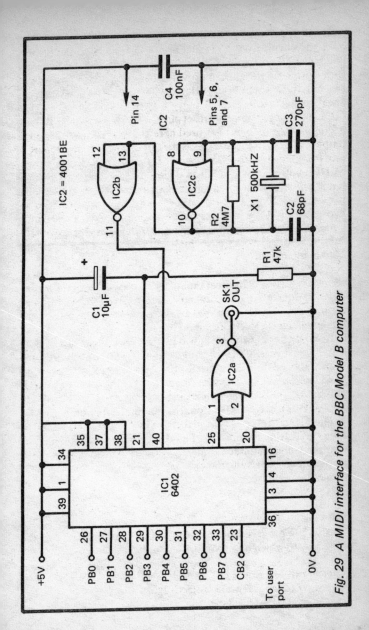

Fig. 29 A MIDI interface for the BBC Model B computer

93

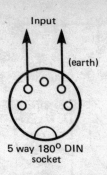

Fig. 30 The connections to the MIDI input socket

| C3 | 270pF ceramic |
| C4 | 100nF ceramic |

*Semiconductors*
| IC1 | 6402 |
| IC2 | 4001BE |

*Miscellaneous*
| SK1 | 5 way DIN socket |
| X1 | 500kHz crystal or ceramic resonator |

40 pin DIL IC holder
14 pin DIL IC holder
Computer connector and Cable
5 way DIN cable
Circuit board, case, etc.

**Software**

This simple program for the BBC model B computer shows the basic way in which notes are written to the instrument.

```
10 ?&FE6C=160
20 ?&FE62=255
30 READ A,B
```

```
40 IF A=0 THEN END
50 ?&FE60=150:?&FE60=A:?&FE60=127
60 FOR D=1 TO B:NEXT
70 ?&FE60=133:?&FE60=A:?&FE60=0
80 GOTO 30
90 DATA 60,500,62,500,64,500,65,500,67,500,69,
     500,71,500,72,1000,0,0
```

Line 10 sets CB2 for the correct operating mode, and line 20 sets PB0 to PB7 as outputs. Note (A) and duration (B) values are READ at line 30 from the DATA statement at line 90. The sample values give a rising scale of C major starting at middle C, but these could obviously be replaced with any desired values. The final two values must be 0, and this ends the sequence properly at line 40 rather than just letting the program crash to a halt. The notes are gated on at line 50, and we are using channel 7 here, but any channel would be suitable and the channel number is then irrelevant. The FOR..NEXT loop at line 60 sets the duration of each note before it is gated off at line 70. The program is looped by line 80 until the sequence is halted.

This simple program should give you the general idea of the way in which sequencing can be accomplished via a MIDI interface. For multichannel sequencing it would be preferable to use machine code so as to obtain better synchronisation between channels. When using BASIC there is no danger of one byte being fed to the interface before the previous one has been processed, but the higher speed of machine code does open up this possibility. One way around the problem would be to monitor the TBRE (transmitter buffer register empty) output at pin 22 of IC1. This goes high when the buffer is empty and the device is ready for the next byte of data. Together with suitable software this could provide a suitable hold-off action. However, in practice it would probably be easier to use a timing loop to space out bytes of data by around $350\mu s$.

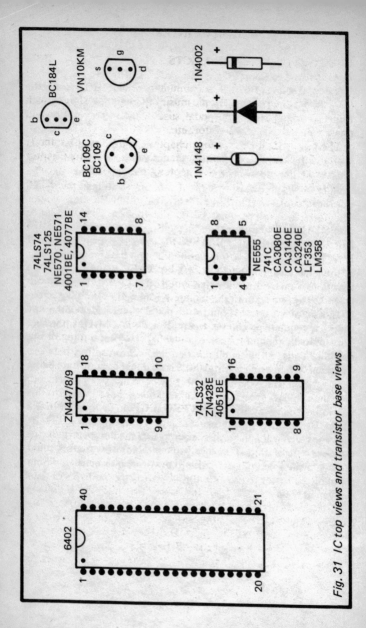

Fig. 31 IC top views and transistor base views

96

**ELECTRONIC MUSIC PROJECTS**                    **BP74**
**R.A. Penfold**
Provides the constructor with a number of practical circuits for the less complex items of electronic music equipment, including such things as fuzz box, waa-waa pedal, sustain unit, reverberation and phaser units, tremelo generator, etc.

The text is divided into four chapters as follows: Chapter 1, Guitar Effects Units; Chapter 2, General Effects Units; Chapter 3, Sound Generator Projects; Chapter 4, Accessories.

*0 900162 94 5*          *112 pages*          *1980*          **£2.50**

**MORE ADVANCED**                                **BP174**
**ELECTRONIC MUSIC PROJECTS**
**R.A. Penfold**
Intended to complement the first book (BP74) by carrying on where it left off and providing a range of slightly more advanced and complex projects. Included are popular effects units such as flanger, phaser, mini-chorus and ring-modulator units. Some useful percussion synthesisers are also described and together these provide a comprehensive range of effects including drum, cymbal and gong-type sounds.

*0 85934 148 8*          *128 pages*          *1986*          **£2.95**

**ELECTRONIC SYNTHESISER PROJECTS**              **BP81**
**M.K. Berry**
Although an electronic synthesiser is quite a complex piece of electronic equipment, it can be broken down into much simpler units which may be built individually and these can then be used or assembled together to make a complete instrument.

This book does just that and is divided into the following chapter headings: 1, Analogue Delay Line; 2, Single Chip Synthesiser; 3, Programmable Sequencer; 4, Voltage-controlled Oscillator; 5, Two VCOs; 6, A.D.S.R. Envelope Shaper; 7, Power Supply Unit; 8 Putting It All Together.

*0 85934 056 2*          *96 pages*          *1981*          **£1.75**

**ELECTRONIC MUSIC**                                    **BP51**
**AND CREATIVE TAPE RECORDING**
**M.K. Berry**

This book sets out to show how electronic music can be made at home with the simplest and most inexpensive of equipment. It then describes how the sounds are generated and how these may be recorded to build up the final composition. For the constructor, several ideas are given to enable him to build up a small studio including a mixer and various sound-effects units.

*0 900162 72 4*          *96 pages*          *1978*          **£2.50**

Please note following is a list of other titles that are available in our range of Radio, Electronics and Computer Books.

These should be available from all good Booksellers, Radio Component Dealers and Mail Order Companies.

However, should you experience difficulty in obtaining any title in your area, then please write directly to the publisher enclosing payment to cover the cost of the book plus adequate postage.

If you would like a complete catalogue of our entire range of Radio, Electronics and Computer Books then please send a Stamped Addressed Envelope to:

BERNARD BABANI (publishing) LTD
THE GRAMPIANS
SHEPHERDS BUSH ROAD
LONDON W6 7NF
ENGLAND